FOX NEWS NUTS?

UNFAIR + UNBALANCED

(for over 200 years)

KRISTINA TOWNSEND

DEDICATION

TO

ROSA MAE BOND

The wind beneath many wings!

TABLE OF CONTENTS

TABLE OF CONTENTS

Preface

I have always considered myself not one for politics. To me, it has always been a boring subject. After all, who cares who wins an election? Regardless to what party they're from, in my mind, politicians are all the same. The only thing I really knew about politics was Democrats and Republicans. What's the difference? As far as I can remember, my family always voted Democratic. I heard rumors to the effect Republicans are for the rich and Democrats are for the poor (and middle-class). At the time, my family was poor. But poor in the United States of America means, you live in a low-income neighborhood. And that we did!

By the time I was old enough to vote, I blindly followed the family tradition of voting Democratic. Although, most of the time I had no idea who I was voting for or what they stood for. I always fell back on, "Republicans were for the rich!" In my mind, all Republicans were rich white people. At the time, we had upper-class, middle-class and lower-class. I thought the upper-class were Republicans and everyone else, Democrats. That was the extent of me and politics! That's all I ever really cared to know. But like I said, I was young. And one of my favorite parts of life as a young person, I could count on a hefty tax return; typically over $1500.

However, during either the late-Reagan years or the early-George H. W. Bush years, that all came to a screeching halt. I all of a sudden started owing over $1500 on my tax return. How could this be when I wasn't making more money than I did the previous year? What happened? This freaked me out! I use to do my own return on the easy form. Maybe I counted wrong? I redid my return twice with the same result. There is a negative number on that bottom field. This means I somehow owe money that I don't have. I had to make payment schedules to get the ball rolling. But before I could payoff that first tax debt, the next year was due.

This cycle kept up for several years until I was way over my head in back taxes. And I never knew what happened until I mentioned it one day at work and someone off in the distance yelled, "Republicans!" Huh? Is that what happened, Republicans? Yes!

As it turned out, one of those Republican guys raised taxes on the middle-class. I think I heard it was Ronald Reagan. But I liked Ronald Reagan. Why exactly? I don't know. I probably liked every president until they got into some big scandal. Like Richard M. Nixon and that Watergate thing I never really understood.

I remember those famous five words, *"I am not a crook!"* Is that what people were calling him? I really didn't know. Nor did I really care. But that was before my tax problem magically appeared. As I struggled to pay my federal taxes down, it never occurred to me to learn more about politics! After about 15-years, I eventually got it all taken care of by getting married and buying real estate. Oh! After all these years, all I needed was deductions and write-offs? I really got out of the rut by refinancing real estate property a few times and including my back taxes in the debts I wanted to payoff. Yippee! Yappie! Yahooey!!!

I still didn't know much more about politics. It seemed to me, an elusive area only a few people really understood. Those people we call "politicians." Was there a class these people took to become politicians? In school, we learned about how the government works and all but real life politics seem like a whole different animal. My logic eventually became, if you can't beat'em (in this case, the rich Republicans who kept raising my taxes), join them! Or at least, try to. Not that I really wanted to be a Republican as much as I wanted to join the upper-class. But I didn't understand much about how different types of income are taxed.

Recently, the whole world magically changed! An African-American Senator from the State of Illinois named, Barack Hussein Obama, announced he was running for the office of the President of the United States of America. Whoever heard of that? Personally, I wished him luck because my only concern was his first name wasn't "Reverend." You know, like Reverend Jessie Jackson and Reverend Al Sharpton. Although, I respect them in the Civil Rights arena, I really didn't take either of them serious as presidential candidates. Then again, Ronald Reagan was once an actor. But that was way before my time and he left acting long before politics. I think.

This young African-American Senator, with boyish charm, charisma and magnetism for days, left the starting gate. When he did that, something I never noticed before happened. It seemed as though every white bigot in the country came out of the woodworks. And that wasn't all. The African-American community suddenly had to struggle with the thought of supporting a serious African-American candidate for the very first time in their lives. This was not an easy transition. Nor was it easy for Barack Obama to convince them, *"Yes We Can!"* In time, African-Americans came around but those white bigots have not changed one bit. I couldn't believe it!

I had seen old pictures from the late fifties of a then 15-year old *Elizabeth Eckford* being followed and threatened by an angry white mob trying to discourage her from entering the all white Little Rock Central High School. I also saw old civil rights footage when police attacked peaceful black marchers with water hoses, police dogs and baton beatings during the Rev. Dr. Martin Luther King, Jr. era. But this was all old footage and photos from over 50-years ago. White people don't think like that anymore. Do they? I found out for sure after Barack Obama shook the gates of white superiority.

As I could not help but to notice the obvious bigotry directed at Barack Obama, I began to document it as I searched deeper to try to understand it. It seemed as though those angry white mobs from 1957, magically appeared in the 2008. They pulled every dirty trick in the book and threw everything including the kitchen sink at this man to try to prevent him from becoming the first African-American President of the United States just like they did little Elizabeth Eckford when she wanted to attend an all white high school. I thought people were suppose to evolve. But this particular breed behaves the exact same way as they always have. Who exactly are they? Why do they remain so stagnate?

As I collected data, I began noticing certain patterns that eventually answered my questions. Who these people are and why they never change. And why they want everything in this country to stay the same. This technically means, working in their favor and no one else's.

In The Beginning ...

In order to understand the American politics of today, I went back as far as I could to understand the American politics of yesterday; then try to connect-the-dots. Today, American politics are primarily divided into two political parties: *Democrats* and *Republicans*. But has it always been that way? This unique endeavor proved quite interesting and very informative. So, fasten your seatbelts!

Throughout the First Party System era (1792 and 1824), two political parties battled for control of the presidency, Congress, and the states. The first of the first political parties, the *Democratic-Republican Party* (1791-1825) was created by *Thomas Jefferson* and *James Madison.* It favored:

- *Republicanism* (liberty [individuals control their own actions], *unalienable rights* [natural: not subject to the laws; legal: bestowed by the legal system]),
- *Jeffersonian Democracy* (equality for every U.S. citizen),
- a *small central government* (controlled by the states)
- *States' rights* (the individual states govern themselves),
- a *strict interpretation* of the U.S. Constitution.

It's rival (the second political party), the *Federalist Party* (1794-1829) was founded by *Alexander Hamilton.* In contrast to the Democratic-Republican Party, this organization favored:

- a *strong central government* (to oversee the individual states),
- a rather *loose interpretation* of the U.S. Constitution.

For 30-years, these two powerhouses met in the political coliseum, known as Congress, to battle for supremacy! But for most of that time, the Democratic-Republican Party controlled Congress and the presidency! Now, fast-forward to their end-of-days; the 1824 presidential election. The drama transpired when four candidates of the Democratic-Republican Party (Andrew Jackson, John Q. Adams, Henry Clay and William H. Crawford) decided to run for the office of President of the United States, simultaneously.

FYI: There was no presidential candidate from the Federalist Party. They had not had a candidate since (Senator) *Rufus King* (NY) was humiliated by the Democratic-Republican candidate, Secretary of State *James*

Monroe with a 183 to 34 electoral college vote landslide victory in the 1816 presidential election. In addition, the Federalist Party has only ever won one presidential election; when Vice-President *John Adams* barely defeated (Secretary of State) *Thomas Jefferson* by a narrow-margin of 71 to 68 electoral college votes in 1796; they needed 70 electoral college votes to win. I can only imagine by the 1824 presidential election the Federalist Party had given up trying to win the presidency!

Having four candidates from the same party run simultaneously with no opposition from a rival party was unprecedented. Then again, there had only been nine presidential elections prior to this one and I'm not sure the first one (where George Washington ran unopposed and was unanimously elected) counts! The severe competition and hostile infighting that emerged during the 1824 presidential campaign season caused the Democratic-Republican Party to splinter into two separate factions. And to make matters worse, after the general election neither of the candidates won the **131** electoral college vote majority needed to win. So, the decision to choose the next President of the United States was left up to the House of Representatives! The final count was as follows:

	Popular	Electoral College	Popular Vote Percentage
Andrew Jackson:	151,271	**99**	41.4%
John Q. Adams:	113,122	84	30.9%
William H. Crawford:	40,856	41	11.2%
Henry Clay:	47,531	37	13.0%

Despite the fact Andrew Jackson came in first-place winning 99 electoral college votes, the House of Representatives gave the presidency to the second runner-up, John Q. Adams! And soon after, Adams appointed Henry Clay as his new Secretary of State. It became obvious to Jackson (and many others), Adams and Clay made a *corrupt bargain* to steal the presidency. In other words, Henry Clay, the then Speaker of the House of Representatives, used all of his power and influence to appoint John Q. Adams to the presidency over Andrew Jackson in return for his appointment to the office of Secretary of State. Incidentally, in those days, the offices of President and Vice-President were not running mates. And fortunately for Jackson, *John C. Calhoun* (a loyal Jackson supporter) won the vice-presidency.

This "corrupt bargain" business to me sounds exactly like the behavior I've come to expect from the extreme Rightwing. It reminds me of the questionable activities that took place during the 2000 George W. Bush [R] versus Al Gore [D] presidential election; where a corrupt bargain was allegedly made to give the presidency to George W. Bush. With that in mind, I am convinced *Henry Clay* (but not so much John Q. Adams) is the forefather of what has become known today as the Rightwing movement in American politics. But let's not stop here but rather keep exploring to find more evidence to support this conclusion. To say the least, I want to be "fair and balanced."

The infighting within the Democratic-Republican Party led to the creation of the Second Party System (1824-1854). The faction led by the very peeved and felt cheated Andrew Jackson splintered off and became the *National Democratic Party* or just the *Democratic Party* (1824-Present). This new northern-based group became the eventual home of the Federalist Party-ers after their organization dissolved five years later in 1829. The remaining Democratic-Republicans, led by John Q. Adams and Henry Clay, became the new southern-based *National Republican Party* or just the *Republican Party* (1824-1833). It appears the two factions split the name of the original organization, as well.

However, as fate would have it, the southern-based National Republican Party only lasted eight years. Dare we say, *"political karma"* for Adam's and Clay? However, to fill the vacuum, Henry Clay quickly formed his version of the *British Whig Party* that favored the supremacy of Parliament over the king, opposing tyranny! By comparison, Clay's *Whig Party* (1833-1854/officially dissolved in 1860) supported the supremacy of Congress over the presidency. And please note, although the members of the Whig Party wore wigs, it had nothing to do with the party's name as much as it was a fashion statement. But it would've been a cool thing to wear wigs that symbolized an opposition to (standing your ground against) tyranny.

On this note, let the records show, *Henry Clay* is the forefather of the *"tyrannical government"* ideal that we hear so much from today's extreme Rightwing! So, as far as I'm concerned, Henry Clay is the forefather of today's Rightwing movement! But let's not stop here. Let's keep digging to see if there's more evidence to support this conclusion. After all, I want to be as "fair and balanced" as I possibly can!

As fate would again have it for the Henry Clay movement, 21-years after its founding, the Whig Party collapsed over the idea of expanding slavery into the federal territories (land overseen by the federal government versus the individual states). Whig politicians were severely divided on this issue. Apparently, some Whigs did not embrace all of Clay's ideals. Coincidentally, as the southern-based Whig Party collapsed in 1854, the new northern-based Republican Party emerged more specifically to challenge expanding slavery into federal territories.

Let me take a moment to review this federal territory issue. Once upon a time (in the early 1800s), the United States consisted of 25 eastern states divided between free states (north) and slave states (south). In 1800, the country of France owned the central region (west of the then United States); a vast territory that is now Arkansas, Missouri, Iowa, Oklahoma, Kansas, Nebraska; one-third of Minnesota; (most of) North Dakota, (most of) South Dakota, northeastern New Mexico; northern Texas, the portions of Montana, Wyoming, and Colorado east of the Continental Divide (a mountainous region stretching from north to south that separates the water systems that drain west into the Pacific Ocean from those that east drain into the Atlantic), and Louisiana west of the Mississippi River. Don't try to visualize it! Just know France owned it!

That is until the 1803 Louisiana Purchase; a land deal where the U.S. federal government purchased the French territories for $15-million ($234-million in today's economy); about 42¢ per acre. Because of wars and such, France had to unload the territory, quickly. After the purchase, the free states and slave states squabbled over whether or not slavery would be permitted in the new territories. That brings us up to speed!

Between 1855-1860, most Whig politicians dropped completely out of politics. But the few who did not, along with the Whig minions who <u>supported</u> the expansion of slavery (the majority), migrated to the Democratic Party. This was to oppose the Whig politicians and minions who <u>opposed</u> extending slavery into the federal territories joining the Republican Party. As a matter of fact, *Abraham Lincoln,* a former Whig leader, became the face of the Republican Party;

4

and eventually the 16th President of the United States. However, many of the former-Whig minions (who joined the Republican Party) became notorious as *"Radical Republicans"*. They can be depicted as a sane version of the Tea Party. Their demands were considered extreme at the time but reasonable by today's standards. They championed things like:

- ending of slavery, completely
- distrusting ex-Confederates with a passion
- harsh penalties for the former Confederate rebels
- civil rights for everyone, equally, regardless of color/race
- voting rights for all free men, regardless of color/race
- former slave owners not be compensated after ending slavery
- limiting voting rights for ex-Confederates
- limiting participation in politics for ex-Confederates

And surprisingly enough, President Lincoln was against everything the Radical Republicans demanded, give or take. For instance, he was against slave-owners owning slaves but he felt they should be compensated for their loses once slavery had been abolished.

Masquerade!

The earliest sign of the demographic known today as "Rightwing" made up as much as three-fourths of the southern-based Whig Party, founded by Senator Henry Clay of Kentucky. As stated in the previous chapter, the Whig Party was split between those who supported the expansion of slavery (the majority) and those who opposed the expansion of slavery (the minority). More specially, today's Rightwing can be traced back to those former-Whigs who supported the expansion of slavery and later joined the Democratic Party. Why didn't they just form their own political party? I have an answer, but I want to build up to it.

By 1855, the northern Democratic and Republican parties were the only two remaining political parties; or at least two most dominant. The former-Whigs who opposed the expansion of slavery naturally gravitated to the Republican Party that was formed on that very principle. Perhaps, joining the Democratic Party as the only option, out of spite, or a combination thereof, was the basic motivation of those former-Whigs who supported the expansion of slavery. Even though the northern-based Democratic Party did not share the same political views as the former-Whigs. As a result, the Democratic Party now had two factions, the north and the south. But technically, the Whigs were only masquerading as Democrats!

The northern Republican Party had very liberal views, as well. They favored abolitionism (ending slavery) and promoted a modernized economy for every U.S. citizen to prosper and pursue the American dream. Hence, the Republican and Democratic Parties shared many of the same views and had similar goals and interests. Even though the former-Whigs who hide themselves within the Democratic party made it substantially bigger than the Republican Party, kept their former views (of expanding slavery) and interests (States' rights). By today's standards, they would be called, *"Democrats In Name Only (DINOs)"*.

These former-Whigs (DINOs) were the segregationist (separatist) element that brought division and infighting to the Democratic Party. They joined the Democratic Party without embracing any of the Democratic principles! DINOs still believed in their old States rights' and smaller government philosophies and were still pro-slavery! Among other things, the northern Republicans and Democrats were abolitionists (who endorsed ending the practice of slavery). But the former-Whigs now within the Democratic Party were segregationists who believed in the separation of the races and profited (by any means necessary) from the barbaric practice of slave labor.

Yep! The more I learn about those Whigs, the more they resemble today's Rightwing movement. And here's that answer I wanted to build up to. The former-Whig southerners did not form their own political party because it was more beneficial for them to join the northern Democratic Party to take advantage of being called a "Democrat" but at the same time not letting go of their former Whig beliefs. Masquerade!

The emergence of the northern Republican Party in 1854 was the beginning of the Third Party System. Although the Democratic Party part of that system had been around since the beginning of the Second Party System that began when it was founded in 1824.

Signs of Rebellion?

Six years later, it was time for the 1860 presidential election. The Democratic Party elected *Stephen A. Douglas* (of Illinois) during the Primaries to run against the Republican candidate, *Abraham Lincoln* (of Illinois). Since Democrats outnumbered Republicans, everyone thought Douglas was a sure win! Perhaps, in an ideal world Douglas was a sure win. But unfortunately (for the Democrats), they didn't live in an ideal world.

As previously mentioned, the former-Whigs who joined the Democratic Party did not embrace Democratic principles. This began to manifest more clearly during the 1860 presidential campaign season. Although the former-Whigs held on to their pro-slavery and states' rights ideals, by 1860, they came up with a few more to add to the list. To name a few:

- *anti-Popular sovereignty* (against putting the expansion of slavery on the voting ballot to let the people decide);
- *secession* (the southern states seceding the union known as the United States of America).

Since the Republican candidate, Abraham Lincoln, opposed the expansion of slavery and secession of southern states from the union, and the Democratic candidate, Stephen Douglas, supported popular sovereignty (putting the expansion of slavery on the voting ballot to let the voters decide), and together they both opposed everything Southern Democrats basically stood for, the Southern Democrats got desperate enough to secede from the main (northern) Democratic Party, form their own party, the *(Southern) Democratic Party* and elect their own candidate, *John C. Breckinridge (Ky)*, to champion their southern ideals:

- expansion of slavery to federal territories
- states' rights (independent states)
- smaller government (no federal government overlords)
- secession (from the United States of America)
- anti-popular sovereignty (their issues on the voting ballot)
- segregation (keeping the races isolated from each other)

Unfortunately for Democrats on both sides (the northerners and the southerners), this meant splitting the Democratic ticket and thus splitting the Democratic vote. But as the voting record for the election stands:

	Popular	Electoral College	Popular Vote Percentage
Abraham Lincoln:	1,865,908	**180**	39.7%
John C. Breckinridge:	848,019	72	18.2%
John Bell:	590,901	39	12.6%
Stephen A. Douglas:	1,380,202	12	29.5%

Many U.S. history buffs think the north and south Democratic split was the reason the Republican candidate, Abraham Lincoln, won the election. But further examination reveals, had the split not occurred, Douglas would have won the popular vote 2,228,221 to Lincoln's 1,865,908. Howbeit, Lincoln still would have won the electoral college vote by a landslide 180 to 84. FYI: **152** electoral college votes were needed to win.

I know you're wondering, *"Who was John Bell?"*, right? He was the candidate of the newly formed *Constitutional Union Party* (1860) created just for that one presidential election. It's members were former-Whig conservatives who actually wanted to avoid secession of southern states from the union over the slavery issue. And surprisingly enough, he did better than the northern Democratic candidate, Stephen A. Douglas, with a whopping 39 electoral college votes! And even more surprising than that, the Southern Democrat candidate, John C. Breckinridge, came in second behind Lincoln (with 72 electoral college votes)! As it turns out, the former-Whigs, were large in voting numbers but they were divided on the secession issue. And the election could very well have looked like this:

	Popular	Electoral College	Popular Vote Percentage
Abraham Lincoln:	1,865,908	**180**	39.7%
John C. Breckinridge:	1,438,920	111	30.8%
Stephen A. Douglas:	1,380,202	12	29.5%

I was about to criticize the Southern Democrats for splitting the Democratic ticket until I discovered the Southern Democratic ticket was split between them and the Southern Constitutional Union Democrats. Dare we say, *"political karma"* for the Southern

Democratic Party? But any way you cut it, Lincoln would still have been the victor, even if there were only two candidates in the race:

	Popular	Electoral College	Popular Vote Percentage
Abraham Lincoln:	1,865,908	**180**	39.7%
Stephen A. Douglas:	2,819,122	123	60.3%

It appears to me, the Lincoln campaign came up with (or decided to use) the *"win the most electoral college votes"* strategy!

Sore-Losers?

I've got to give credit where it's due. The Southern Democrats made a noble effort to win the 1860 presidential election. Their candidate came in second behind Abraham Lincoln and did much better than the northern Democratic candidate, who came in last place out of four. Any rational group of people would have made this recognition, accepted it and moved on. But where I fault the Southern Democrats is they did not let it go after Lincoln won the 1860 presidential election fair and square! The hot-headed and unreasonable Southern Democrats' next step was to secede the Union all together and form their own country; *The Confederate States of America*. This now made them, Southern <u>Confederate</u> Democrats; not to be confused with the northern Democratic Party!

To be more specific, in December 1860 (one month after the presidential election), *South Carolina* flew the coop and seceded! A few months later in February 1861, after the other states realized the world did not come to an end, *Alabama, Florida, Georgia, Texas, Louisiana* and *Mississippi* joined in on the secession. They quickly formed a government and selected their own president, *Jefferson Davis.* They even wrote their own Constitution, whose Preamble began, *"We, the people of the Confederate States, each state acting in its sovereign and independent character..."* Yes, they immediately implemented their "states' rights" philosophy.

Now, who exactly was this guy, Jefferson Davis? It sounds like he just sprouted up out of a hole in the ground when the Southern Confederate Democrats needed a leader for their rebellion. But actually, Jefferson Davis was very well-known in American politics! First of all, he was a

9

member of the Democratic Party and held a seat in the House of Representatives from December 1845 to June 1846. Why only 6-months? The Mexican-American war started in late April of 1846 and in June, Jefferson traded-in his congressional seat for a military uniform. He started the volunteer 155th Infantry Regiment that became known as the "Mississippi Rifles" because they were the first regiment to be fully equipped with the latest state-of-the art M1841 Mississippi rifle.

In February 1847, Davis led his regiment in the Battle of Buena Vista, was shot in the foot, carried off the battlefield and never returned. In May 1847, for his bravery on the battlefield, Governor Brown of Mississippi appointed Davis to the U.S. Senate to replace Jesse Speight who passed away; his tenure ended in September 1851. In March 1853, President Franklin Pierce appointed Davis his Secretary of War until March 1857. Davis then returned to the Senate from March 1857 to January 1861.

On secession, he believed each state had the right to secede from the Union but he did not believe they should. He knew the North would not permit the peaceable exercise of the right to secession. Of course they wouldn't! It was an "imaginary right" invented by the South! Regardless, South Carolina was the first to secede in December 1860 and Davis' home state of Mississippi followed in January 1861. This is why he left the Senate. Because of his strong military and political credentials, Jefferson Davis was an easy choice to lead the Confederacy.

The northern Republican and northern Democrat's formed an alliance to force the southern Democratic secession states back into the union. Hence, that's why those guys in the blue uniforms were called, "The Union Army". And as far as those guys in the gray uniforms are concerned, at what point does losing a presidential election mean you win your own country? The main reasons the Confederacy gave for rebelling was the fact the United States government ignored all their state laws regarding slavery.

Shortly after the fighting started (April 14, 1861), *Virginia, North Carolina, Tennessee* and *Arkansas* joined the Confederacy. But the slave states, Missouri, Kentucky, Maryland and Delaware remained loyal to the Union; an indication the war was not primarily about ending slavery. However, on April 9, 1865 (just 5-days shy of 4-years), the Confederate General, Robert E. Lee surrendered to

Union General, Ulysses S. Grant at Appomattox Courthouse, VA. The ending of slavery in the south was merely a byproduct of the northern Republicans and Democrats (abolitionists who wanted the practice of slavery abolished) winning the war. Dare we say, *"political karma"* for the Southern Confederate Democrats?

Once again, any rational demographic would have acknowledged their noble effort to secede the union and try to make it on their own in their own country. But once again, Southern Confederate Democrats (a.k.a. Southern Democrats) did not let it go after they lost the civil war they started! On April 14, 1865 (the 4-year anniversary of when the civil war began; and five days after the war officially ended), a Southern Confederate Democrat assassin, *John Wilkes Booth,* cowardly sneaked up behind President Abraham Lincoln and shot him in the back of his head as he (Lincoln) watched a performance at the Ford's Theater in Washington D.C. Did I mention the fact they're *"sore-losers?"*

So far, we've watched the Rightwing movement evolve through the following political trek:

- Democratic-Republican Party (1791-1825)
- National Republican Party, southern-based (1825-1833)
- Whig Party (1833-1860)
- (National) Democratic Party, northern-based (1855-1860)
- Southern Democratic Party (1860)
- Southern Confederate Democrats (1861-1865)

What next?

Secret Secession

Most people only know a few details surrounding the assassination of President Abraham Lincoln. Some even consider the Southern Confederate Democrats "sore-losers" for killing Lincoln after they lost the civil war "they" started. We all know the name of Lincoln's assassin, but do we know anything about him or his true motivations? Let's examine these details before moving on.

It was no big secret that Southern Democrats (before they became

Confederates) hated Lincoln with a passion but most do not fully understand why. The official versions center around political issues like the expansion of slavery and states' rights but there was more that went on than meets the eye.

In the official version, Abraham Lincoln was the second child of *Thomas Lincoln* and *Nancy Hanks Lincoln*, born February 12, 1809 in a one-room log cabin on the Sinking Spring Farm in Hardin County, Kentucky; the great-great-great-great-grandson of Samuel Lincoln, who arrived in Hingham, Massachusetts, from Norfolk, England, in the 17th century. However, the plot thickens when exploring the unofficial avenues.

In 1938, *Hertz, Emanuel* (a lawyer, historian, and the authority on Abraham Lincoln at the time) published a book titled, *"The Hidden Lincoln, From the Letters and Papers of William H. Herndon"*. FYI: *William Henry Herndon* was the law partner and biographer of Abraham Lincoln. In the book, Herndon claims Thomas Lincoln could not have been Abraham Lincoln's father because he was sterile from childhood mumps and was later castrated. Herndon is further documented as describing Abraham Lincoln had very dark skin and coarse hair because his mother (Nancy Hanks) was from an Ethiopian tribe.

J. A. Rogers (Joel Augustus Rogers), author, journalist, historian, in his 1965 paperback, *"The Five Negro Presidents: According to what White People Said They Were"*, he documents Nancy Hanks, as saying *"Abraham Lincoln was the illegitimate son of an African man"* but she was not the only source of this affirmation. During the 1860 presidential campaign season, among other things, Southern Democrats claimed the Republican candidate, Abraham Lincoln, was a black man! A serious charge back then when bigotry was as natural to Southern Democrats as breathing. As a matter of fact, in political attack ads (Yes, they existed back then), Southern Democrats made cartoon drawings depicting Lincoln as a Negro, nicknaming him, *"Abraham Africanus the First"*.

This may seem trivial to us today, but in the 1850s, if your great-great-great-great-great-great-grandcestor had one teeny weenie drop of African blood, you were considered a black person! They called this the *"one drop rule"* and they were very serious about it! As a matter of fact, there were quite a few slaves at the time who could pass for white people. Many whites (or considered whites) living in southern society had African ancestors. The ones who successfully kept their heritage a secret were accepted as white, but those who did (or could) not or if their secret was later discovered, all rights and privileges of being white were immediately, harshly and cruelly revoked and that person was reduced to property status and treated as a slave!

Abraham Lincoln's alleged African ancestry is a conversation that still continues today but in 1860 Southern Democrats believed it to be true with a passion! Can you imagine how people who believed "blacks should be slaves to the white man" felt when a person they honestly believed was a black man was about to become the next President of the United States? Oh yeah. Of course you can. That happened back in 2008. But try to put yourself in the mid-1800s when the very notion of a black man (considered inferior to whites) leading a country full of white people was not considered possible. This was the driving force behind the way Southern Democrats responded after Abraham Lincoln won the election. Can we say, *"Karma for the Southern Democrats"?*

Be that as it may, Southern Democrats refused to live in a country led by someone they considered an inferior black man. I suppose they ignored the fact the inferior black man just outsmarted them and won the presidential election. So, in their complete humiliation and embarrassment (a trait that seems to follow their endeavors) one by one southern states seceded the Union to form their bigot country, The Confederate States of America; guaranteed to keep black people in a servant status to white bigots!

This brings us back to the place we started out, after the civil war ended. Once again, President Abraham Lincoln was assassinated by John Wilkes Booth. Now, who exactly was he? John Wilkes Booth was a stage actor from a popular theatrical family, The Booths, originally from England. Politically, he was a Southern Confederate Democrat. Booth and many other Confederates believed the civil war was still ongoing, as long as, Confederate soldiers were still fighting Union soldiers. Hence, after Confederate

13

General Robert E. Lee surrendered to Union General Ulysses S. Grant at Appomattox Court House on April 9, 1865, Confederate General Joseph E. Johnston's army was still fighting; but probably because he hadn't heard the war was over.

FYI: Throughout the war, Joseph E. Johnston and Confederate President Jefferson Davis had their own personal civil war. For starters, Johnston resented Davis for appointing Robert E. Lee, and two others, to full general ahead of him. Johnston felt since he was the highest ranking officer (brigadier "1-star" general) among the four in the old regular army and the first to resign and join the Confederacy, he should've been the first to be appointed a full "4-star" general in the Confederate army. Instead, Lee and two others were promoted before Johnston, thus outranking him. On the other hand, Davis resented Johnston for losing most of the battles he was directly in-charge of.

In the same spirit that Lee's nemesis during the war was Grant, Johnston's nemesis was Union Major-General William T. Sherman. Johnston's final battle was against Sherman at the Battle of Bentonville in North Carolina. Longer story short, Johnston fought long and hard but eventually surrendered the Army of Tennessee and all remaining Confederate forces still active in North Carolina, South Carolina, Georgia, and Florida; the largest surrender of the war, over 89,000 soldiers. President Davis felt that Johnston surrendering so many troops that had not been defeated in battle, committed an act of treachery.

Whether the war was officially over when Confederate General Robert E. Lee surrendered to Union General Ulysses S. Grant on April 9th or when Confederate General Joseph E. Johnston surrendered to Union Major-General William T. Sherman on April 26th, John Wilkes Booth was not in the military! He was just a southern Confederate sympathizer who hated the fact the man they considered a black president not only beat them in the 1860 presidential election (and was re-elected in the 1864 presidential election), he had now beat them in all out civil war. A handful of Southern Confederates were determined to not have someone they considered to be a "black president" governing over them. So, that handful of Southern Confederates conspired and murdered the president, whom they claimed was a black man.

Ku Klux Klan

After the civil war had ended the south was in shambles. The victorious northern Republican Congress began what they called, the Reconstruction of the south; issuing policies that established political and economic equality for blacks. Republican coalitions, empowered throughout the southern states endeavored to convert the south by setting up a free labor economy, using the U.S. Army and the Freedmen's Bureau (an organization that protected the legal rights of freedmen, negotiated labor contracts, and set up schools and churches). This encouraged thousands of northerners to go south, as missionaries, teachers, businessmen and politicians. Unfortunately, they were met by hostile and resentful southerners who derogatorily called them *"Carpetbaggers"* because carpet bags was commonly used to carry luggage. They also called southerners who cooperated with the north, *"Scalawags"*, a word originally used to describe worthless livestock.

The fact that their former slaves now held political and military power angered many southern whites. As a result, six veterans of the Confederate army, in Pulaski, Tennessee, founded a terrorist group called the *Ku Klux Klan (KKK);* derived from the Greek word *"kuklos"*, meaning: circle or band (of brothers). The KKK primarily targeted liberal whites (carpetbaggers and scalawags) and politically empowered blacks who cooperated with the Republican Congress' Reconstruction policies. And the fact that black men were given the right to vote in public elections in 1867 only made matters worse. The KKK waged an underground guerilla war campaign of fear, bullying, intimidation, and violence. Even though the Republican Congress passed legislation intended to curb Klan terrorism, the Klan succeeded in achieving its primary goal of reestablishing white supremacy through (Southern) Democratic victories in state legislatures throughout the southern states.

In this regard, the northern Republican reconstruction era was considered a complete failure. But how could it succeed when hostile southerners crept around at night inflicting guerilla warfare tactics on innocent and defenseless people that included (but were not limited to): kidnapping, murder, rape, lynching, bombings, arson, and cross-burnings when the civil war was supposedly over?

And then they cry, *"God Bless America!"* FYI: These were the same type of people who criticized Rev. Jeremiah Wright for saying, *"God dam America!"* as though there's never a good reason to say that. But I bet the people who fell victim to the KKK's terrorist tactics with seemingly no help from federal authorities at the time (laws took time to enforce) would agree with Rev. Wright.

On that note, this 1865 Ku Klux Klan was only the first version to pop up in American history. Its members were unmistakable dawning white robes, masks, and pointed hats (later versions wore pointed hoods that covered the face), designed to be shocking and terrifying, and to hide their identities. They would blend in society by day then ride around terrorizing by night. By 1871, the federal government passed the *Force Acts* (three bills designed to protect the blacks' right to vote, hold political office, serve on juries, and receive the equal protection under the law), which were used to prosecute KKK crimes. Prosecution of Klan crimes and enforcement of the Force Acts suppressed Klan activity until the organization completely faded out (by 1873).

Unfortunately (for blacks and white Republicans) by 1874, newly organized and openly active paramilitary groups, such as the White League and the Red Shirts, started a fresh round of violence aimed at keeping blacks from voting or holding political office and voting white Republicans out of office. Basically, picking up where the Ku Klux Klan left off, the terrorist tactics of these groups contributed to segregationist white (former-Confederate) Democrats regaining political power in all the Southern states by 1877. And because of a national compromise with the northern Republican Party to gain Southern support in the intensely disputed 1876 presidential election, federal troops were withdrawn from state politics in the South (ending the Reconstruction era). This made it easy for Southern Democrats to begin institutionalizing Jim Crow laws (mandating racial segregation in all public facilities in Southern states of the former Confederacy) throughout the south.

As it turned out, racism was big business! In 1915, six more men swore an allegiance to the reborn Ku Klux Klan; a second Klan was founded in Atlanta-GA. But it wasn't until 1921 that the group adopted a modern business system of recruiting. This was the beginning of the Roaring twenties decade where prosperity was everywhere; at least for whites. Recruits of the new Klan paid an initiation fee and they paid for the costumes they would eventually wear as commissions to the organizers. Chi-Ching! The movement rapidly grew nationwide reflecting the social tensions of urban industrialization and increased immigration. The membership grew most rapidly in big cities, and spread out of the South to the Midwestern and Western regions. The KKK's message included 100% Americanism, demanded the purification of politics, called for strict morality, and better enforcement of prohibition. The official rhetoric focused on the threat of the Catholic Church, endorsing anti-Catholicism and nativism (opposition to immigration).

This version of the Ku Klux Klan was a formal fraternity with a national and state structure. At its peak in the mid-1920s, it boasted 15% of the nation's eligible white male population (between four and five million). But contrary to the group's message, internal divisions, criminal behavior by leaders (including sexual assaults on women), and external opposition brought about a decline in membership. To add coals to the fire, the 1929 stock market crash and the 1930's great depression helped close the book on this chapter of the Ku Klux Klan.

By 1950, the U.S. economy was getting back to normal and so was racism. The Ku Klux Klan name was used by numerous white supremacist groups that opposed the Civil Rights movement, the desegregation of the south and the abolishment of Jim Crow laws. Despite all their terrorist activity, Civil Rights legislation was passed, desegregation of the south was enacted and Jim Crow laws were abolished. Today, it is estimated there are about 150 independent Ku Klux Klan chapters with about 5,000 members, nationwide. But they have a lot of competition from other white supremacist hate groups, such as (but not limited to):

- American Nazi Party
- Aryan Brotherhood
- Assembly of Christian Soldiers
- European Kindred
- Friends of New Germany
- Hammerskins

- Knights of the White Camelia
- Nazi Lowriders
- The Order
- Posse Comitatus
- Red Shirts
- Redneck Shop
- Supreme Order of Caucasians
- United Klans of America
- White Aryan Resistance
- White League
- White Patriot Party

Civil Wrongs?

Where are we now? The year, 1876. White supremacist groups (beginning with the Ku Klux Klan) ran rampant and lawless in the former Confederate southern states targeting politically empowered blacks and the white Republicans who helped them gain such equality; Southern (Confederate) Democratic politicians took over state and local level politics, enforcing Jim Crow laws that segregated blacks from whites in public places, calling it "Separate but Equal" but was really "Separate and Unequal". And to top everything off, the wake of the *1876 presidential election* that sealed the fate of (and ended) the Reconstruction era that began in 1865 after the civil war ended. What happened exactly?

The 23rd quadrennial presidential election between Republican candidate *Rutherford B. Hayes* of Ohio and Democratic candidate *Samuel J. Tilden* of New York is among the most controversial in American history; the results of which remain among the most disputed ever. It was a very close race. There is no question Tilden outpolled Hayes in the popular vote and after a first count, it was clear that Tilden had won 184 electoral votes to Hayes's 165, with 20 votes unresolved. These 20 electoral votes were in dispute in four states: Florida, Louisiana, South Carolina, and Oregon. In the first three, each party reported its candidate had won the state. But in Oregon, one elector was declared illegal and was replaced. The question of who should have been awarded these electoral votes is the source of the continued controversy concerning the results of this election.

As a result, an informal deal called the *Compromise of 1877* was struck to resolve the dispute; this awarded all 20 electoral votes to Hayes. In return for the Southern Democrats' acquiescence (unfairly award Hayes the 20 electoral college votes) Republicans agreed to withdraw federal troops from the former Confederate states in the south; thus, ending Reconstruction. This Compromise effectively ceded political power in the Southern states to the Democratic politicians who called themselves, Redeemers (of the south). Although Tilden won 50.9% of the popular vote to Hayes's 47.9%, Hayes won the election with 185 electoral college votes to Tilden's 184; 185 electoral college votes was needed to win.

As the federal troops packed their bags and exodused the south, many white Republicans left with them and southern blacks felt abandoned and betrayed. Southern blacks called the compromise *"The Great Betrayal"* because they were left at the mercy of the same southern white bigots who had been subjecting them to kidnappings, rapes, lynching and murder. And this is one of those occasions where blacks were screaming, *"God dam America!"*

The Jim Crow laws were blatant racial segregation laws enacted in the former Confederate states at the state and local levels. This separation in practice led to conditions for southern blacks that tended to be inferior to those provided for southern whites. And because of the compromise made between northern Republicans and southern Democrats, black southerners would suffer under the cruel hand of white superiority for the nearly 90-years.

States' Rights Democratic Party

In 1948, the 41st quadrennial presidential election was held between three candidates: *Harry S. Truman* [Democrat], *Thomas E. Dewry* [Republican], and *Storm Thurmond* [Dixiecrat]. What's a Dixiecrat? Let's start from the beginning and work our way up.

First off, this election is considered to be the greatest election upset in American history; every prediction indicated the Democratic incumbent, Harry S. Truman, would be defeated by the

Republican challenger, Thomas E. Dewey. Truman's surprise victory was the fifth consecutive presidential win for the Democratic Party, the longest winning streak in the party's history. But how did all of this come about?

In December of 1946, President Truman by executive order established the *President's Committee on Civil Rights (PCCR)* who's goal was to investigate the status of civil rights in the country; then propose measures to strengthen and protect them. In October of 1947, *"To Secure These Rights: The Report of the President's Committee on Civil Rights"* was delivered to the president; this 178-page report proposed improving existing civil rights laws. More specifically, the report aimed to establish a permanent Civil Rights Commission, a Joint Congressional Committee on Civil Rights, and a Civil Rights Division in the Department of Justice, to develop federal protection from lynching, among other things. Finally, in July of 1948, President Truman advanced the recommendations of the report by signing Executive Orders 9980 and 9981; ordering the desegregation of the federal work force and the desegregation of the armed services, respectively.

In his younger years, President Truman served as an artillery man in World War I. As a soldier him realized the horrors of war; this caused him gain a respect for soldiers. So, President Truman was appalled when he heard stories of African-American World War II veterans being mistreated in the southern states, shortly after returning home. This particular case caught his attention: *Isaac Woodard*, a black sergeant who was honorably discharged from the U.S. army in 1946 (after being awarded a Battle Star, Good Conduct Medal, Service Medal, and a Victory Medal) was beaten and maimed just hours after returning home, losing both his eyes in the process. His attacker, South Carolina Police Chief *Linwood Shull*, openly admitted he used excessive force. But despite all the evidence against Shull, he was acquitted of all charges in front of an all-white jury. This is why southern bigots never think their actions will have consequences. The consequence they didn't see coming was President Truman revamping and enforcing civil rights!

President Truman's decision to desegregate the armed forces and federal workforce came 100-days before the 1948 presidential election. This was the main reason everyone predicted Truman would lose the election to the Republican challenger. Another reason Truman was expected to lose the election - In a panic and afraid they were about to lose their southern (segregated) way of life (and ignoring the fact it was at their own doing), Southern Democrats decided to secede the main northern-based Democratic Party and form their own party, *"The States' Rights Democratic Party."* In addition, they were given the moniker *"Dixie Democrats"* to distinguish Democrats south of the Mason-Dixon line from Democrats north of the Mason-Dixon line; which was shortened to *"Dixiecrats".* The Dixiecrat candidate, Governor of South Carolina, *Storm Thurmond.* Hence, everyone thought the Democratic vote would be split between Truman and Thurman, paving the way for Republican Thomas E. Dewry to win the election.

As it turned out, *Harry S. Truman* won the 1948 presidential election by a landslide! He won a whopping 49.6% of the popular vote and 303 electoral college votes; 266 electoral college votes were needed to win. In comparison, the Republican challenger, *Thomas E. Dewry* won 45.1% of the popular vote and 189 electoral college votes. And the Dixiecrat challenger, *Storm Thurmond,* won 2.4% of the popular vote and 39 electoral college votes! Can we say, *"Karma for the Southern Democrats"* boys and girls? In addition, this election established the northern-based Democratic Party's status as the nation's majority party.

As a result of the shocking way things turned out in the 1948 presidential election, the vast majority of Southern Democrats were completely embarrassed, humiliated and furious over the fact their southern (segregated) way of life's days were now numbered. And in their raging fit, the majority refused to return to the northern-based Democratic Party. However, a few politicians in strategic positions returned so they could hinder the party from within (which still continues today). But the vast majority of the Dixiecrat minions migrated to the northern-based Republican Party, instead. This migration took place gradually between the end of 1948 to about 1954. Long story short, today the Southern (Confederate) Democrats have completely taken over the northern-based Republican Party, still waving and displaying the Confederate flag as they try to change the image of Abraham Lincoln, who spent his entire presidency fighting against the Confederate flag and whom their predecessors eventually murdered.

Civil Rights, The Movement

When President Harry S. Truman signed Executive Order 9981 in July of 1948, desegregating the armed services, this catapulted a series of events that would become known as the *Civil Rights Movement*. This action was actually the direct result of Southern Democrats harassing, bullying, threatening, intimidating, beating, and maiming blacks who returned home to southern states after serving in the military and defended this country fighting in World War II. I am now convinced, southern bigots were just plain evil! In addition to that, they perceive the consequences of their own actions as unfair personal attacks. Thus, they saw no reason for Truman to desegregate anything. Southern Democrats retaliated, immediately after their candidate lost the 1948 presidential election in an embarrassing landslide, by joining the Republican Party; a migration that lasted between 1948 and 1954.

In 1954, six years after the desegregation of the armed services, the Supreme Court ruled on the landmark case, *Brown v. Board of Education of Topeka, Kansas*, in a unanimous agreement that the segregation of public schools was unconstitutional. Since it was a Supreme Court ruling, this meant segregation in every public school was unconstitutional! This landmark ruling overturned the 1896 *Plessy v. Ferguson* ruling that sanctioned *"separate but equal"* segregation of the races, declaring separate educational facilities inherently unequal.

In August 1955, fourteen-year-old *Emmett Till* (of Chicago, IL), while visiting family in Mississippi, was kidnapped, brutally beaten, shot, and dumped in the Tallahatchie River for allegedly whistling at a white woman. Two Southern Democrats, *J. W. Milam* and *Roy Bryant*, were arrested for the murder and acquitted by an all-white Southern Democrat jury. And to add insult to injury, the two later boasted about committing the murder and getting away with it in a Look magazine interview. This incident was the final straw that ignited the civil rights movement. And once again, Southern

Democrats failed to see it was the consequences of their own actions, coming back to haunt them. And for the record, Emmett Till's murderers, J. W. Milam and Roy Bryant die of cancer by 1994.

By December 1955, blacks had become bolder in standing up to the Southern Democratic bigots! For example, in Montgomery-AL, 42-year old *Rosa Louise McCauley Parks* refused to obey bus driver *James F. Blake's* order to give up her seat at the front of the "colored section" of the bus to a white passenger, after the white section was filled. In response to her arrest the Montgomery black community launched a bus boycott, which lasted for more than a year, until the buses were desegregated in December of 1956. The president of the Montgomery Improvement Association (MIA), *Reverend Martin Luther King, Jr.*, lead the boycott.

In January 1957, *Martin Luther King, Charles K. Steele*, and *Fred L. Shuttlesworth (SCLC)* established the *Southern Christian Leadership Conference.* The SCLC became a major force in organizing the civil rights movement and based its principles on nonviolence and civil disobedience. Reverend King taught his members and followers, it was essential that the civil rights movement not sink to the level of the racist Southern Democrats who opposed them.

In September 1957, Southern Democrats still challenged the desegregation of public schools. In Little Rock-AR, Nine black students were blocked from entering formerly all-white Central High School on the orders of *Governor Orval Faubus*. In response, President Eisenhower sent federal troops and the National Guard to intervene on behalf of the students, who become known as the *"Little Rock Nine"*.

In February 1960, Four black students of the North Carolina Agricultural and Technical College in Greensboro began a sit-in at a segregated Woolworth's lunch counter. They were refused service, but allowed to stay at the counter. This event triggered many similar nonviolent protests throughout the South. Six months later the original four protesters were served lunch at the same Woolworth's counter. Student sit-ins became an effective method in integrating parks, swimming pools, theaters, libraries, and other public facilities throughout the Deep South.

In May 1961, student volunteers (a.k.a. freedom riders) sponsored by the *Congress of Racial Equality (CORE)* and the *Student Nonviolent Coordinating Committee (SNCC)*, took bus trips throughout the South to test out new laws that prohibited segregation in interstate travel facilities that included bus and railway stations. Several of the groups were attacked by angry Southern Democrat (now Republican) mobs along the way.

In October 1962, *James Meredith* became the first black student to enroll at the University of Mississippi. Southern Democrats (now Republican) caused violence and riots to erupt surrounding this momentous occasion. In response, President Kennedy to send 5,000 federal troops to police the Southern Democrat (now Republican) racists and hatemongers.

In April 1963, *Martin Luther King* was arrested and incarcerated during peaceful anti-segregation protests in Birmingham-AL. His argument stated, *"Individuals have a moral duty to disobey unjust laws".* The recipients of said unjust laws agreed with him. In May, the *Commissioner of Public Safety Eugene "Bull" Connor* used fire hoses and police dogs on peaceful black demonstrators. King's non-violence strategy worked like a charm! Images of peaceful black demonstrators being brutality attacked by hostile Southern Democrats (now Republicans) were televised and widely published. Thus, the civil rights movement gained worldwide attention, as well as, worldwide sympathy.

In June 1963, NAACP field secretary, Medger Evers, was murdered outside his home at the age of 37. Southern Democrat (now Republican) Byron De La Beckwith was tried twice for the murder in 1964 but got off both times with hung juries. Yes, they were all-white. However, 30-years later, Byron was finally convicted for Evan's murder. Times change, people change.

In August 1963, about 200,000 people join in on the March on Washington and congregated at the Lincoln Memorial to listen to Martin Luther King's now famous *"I Have A Dream"* speech. In September, four young black girls, *Denise McNair, Cynthia Wesley, Carole Robertson,* and *Addie Mae Collins,* were killed while attending Sunday school when a bomb exploded at the Sixteenth

Street Baptist Church; a popular location for civil rights meetings. As a result, riots erupted in Birmingham, leading to the deaths of two more black youths.

In January 1964, the 24th Amendment was ratified to abolish poll tax laws. After the right to vote was extended to all races by the enactment of the 15th Amendment, many Southern states enacted poll tax laws as a means of restricting poor black voters. Today, they use the same tactic with government issued IDs. Anyway, poll tax laws often included a grandfather clause, which allowed any adult male whose father or grandfather had voted in a specific year prior to the abolition of slavery to vote without paying the tax. In other words, the law specifically targeted blacks.

Beginning summer of 1964, the *Council of Federated Organizations (COFO)*, a network of civil rights groups that includes CORE and SNCC, launched a massive effort to register black voters during what became known as the Freedom Summer. The Council also sent delegates to the Democratic National Convention to protest and attempt to unseat the official all-white Mississippi contingent.

In July 1964, President *Lyndon B. Johnson* signed the *Civil Rights Act of 1964*. The most sweeping civil rights legislation since Reconstruction, the Civil Rights Act prohibited discrimination of all kinds based on race, color, religion, or national origin. The law also provided the federal government with the powers to enforce desegregation.

In August 1965, Congress passed the Voting Rights Act of 1965. This did not give blacks the right to vote; they had that since 1867. This voting rights act made it easier for southern blacks to register to vote. Hence, literacy tests, poll taxes, and other underhanded requirements employed by Southern Democrats to restrict black voting was made illegal.

In September 1965, President *Lyndon B. Johnson* issued Executive Order 11246, which enforced affirmative action for the first time. It required government contractors to *"take affirmative action"* toward prospective minority employees in all aspects of hiring and employment. This would not have been necessary if the work force was as fair to blacks as it was to whites. At any rate, this helped level the playing field in hiring practices.

In April 1968, President *Lyndon B. Johnson* signed the *Civil Rights Act of 1968*, prohibiting discrimination in the sale, rental, and financing of housing.

Whew! From 1948 to 1968, legislation from the White House and Congress gradually emerged to right social wrongs that existed in southern American society since 1867. And the vast majority of angry, hostile and abusive Southern Democrats (now Republicans) are oblivious to how much their constantly "on-the-warpath" actions (unintentionally) contributed to making it all possible.

Rightwing Republicans, An Oxymoron?

We have traced the Rightwing attitude from its humble beginnings in American politics to present:

- Democratic-Republican Party (1791-1825)
- National Republican Party, southern-based (1825-1833)
- Whig Party (1833-1860)
- (National) Democratic Party, northern-based (1855-1860)
- Southern Democratic Party (1860)
- Southern Confederate Democrats (1861-1865)
- National Democratic Party (1866-1947)
- States' Rights Democratic Party (1948)
- National Republican Party, northern-based (1948-Present)

Prior to 1960, most (if not all) African-Americans supported the Republican Party. It was seen as the party of Abraham Lincoln, who was perceived as having ended the enslavement of blacks in the southern former-Confederate states. In contrast, they avoided the Democratic Party like a plague because within it resided the Southern Democrats who endorsed segregation and enforced the Jim Crow laws, condemning blacks to second-class citizenship.

Incidentally, when African-Americans realized, out of anger towards Democratic President Harry S. Truman's 1948 desegregation of the armed services, the former-Southern Democrats had now joined the Republican Party, African-Americans, refusing to be in the same political party as the people who hated and oppressed them, joined the Democratic Party in droves! This is why today (2014), most African-Americans are Democrats and most Rightwing advocates are Republicans. The Southern Democrats who over 65-years ago joined to the Republican Party have now completely taken it over! They have gradually transformed the northern-based Republican Party that opposed the Confederate flag into a Republican Party that embraces southern Confederate ideals and proudly waves the Confederate flag. They desecrate the image of Abraham Lincoln who spent his entire presidency fighting against the Confederate flag to one that suggests he now embraces the Confederate flag.

Today, the once liberal Republican Party embraces Rightwing ideals to various degrees. On the end of the spectrum are the *Old School Republicans* who consist mostly of wealthy white males who share liberal views on the social issues but are more conservative on the economic (fiscal) issues. Because this group is wealthy and economic-driven, they are also called the *"Wall Street Republicans".* This group of veterans makes up 22% of the Republican Party. On the opposite end of the spectrum are the *Tea Party Movement Republicans* (a name derived from the Boston Tea Party of 1773); the most conservative and religious segment who holds extremely strong and uncompromising views on all the issues, including but not limited to: reducing the national debt and federal budget deficits by reducing government spending. The Tea Partyers make up 28% of the Republican Party.

Somewhere in-between the two extremes are the *Religious Values Republicans* who are really more moderately religious than the Tea Partyers. Most are females who focus on the country's religious heritage and are conservative on social and economic issues. The Religious Values Republicans make up 21% of the Republican Party. Next are the *Pro-Government Republicans,* who can be described as "highly religious", holds very conservative views on the social issues but are open to the idea of a larger government versus states' rights. The Pro-Government Republicans are a 12% minority. Then there are the *Window Shopper Republicans* who are mostly between the ages of 18 and 29. This is the most liberal group in the bunch and are considered borderline Democrats. The Window Shoppers are 17% of the Republican base.

As you can now see, the extreme Tea Party Movement Republicans make up the largest segment of the Republican Party. Since they have an extreme mentality, they take complete advantage of the fact they outnumber the other groups. So, whatever idea they come up with, regardless to how crazy it might seem to everyone else, the Tea Party leads the charge and the Republican Party has to deal with the fallout. For this reason, internal frays develop when the Tea Party decides to do something that may result in hurting the U.S. economy which will also hurt the Wall Street Republicans' holdings. Hence, the Wall Street Republicans won't stand for that, then one thing leads to another. In addition to that, Republican presidential candidates have to figure out ways to appeal to the different facets of the Republican Party. The trick is to accomplish this without appearing like a flip-flopper (i.e. say one thing to one group and the complete opposite to another group). The last Republican presidential candidate failed miserably.

Now, with so many facets of the Republican Party, who decides the principles, values, ethics core beliefs? Let's go through the list of financial supporters and outside influences:

American Crossroads/Crossroads GPS
These partner organizations are Super PACs (committees that are not allowed to make contributions to the campaign or party of the candidate they support, but are allowed to engage in unlimited spending independently of the campaign and party they support) that take their cues from Republican strategists *Karl Rove* and *Carl Forti*, and former Republican National Committee heads *Haley Barbour*, *Ed Gillespie* and *Mike Duncan*. Combined, these two are considered the heaviest hitter among Republican outside groups. The difference between the groups, Crossroads GPS is required to report what it spends, but it is not required to publicly disclose any donor information.

Americans for Prosperity
The main outlet for libertarian billionaire brothers *Charles Koch* and *David Koch*. In 2010, they helped the budding Tea Party grow in and has spent heavily in support of libertarian-minded Republicans. Because of the way it is structured, it does not have to disclose its donors. However, 2013 tax filings show the group spent $122-million during 2012 but came up short in its bid to make President

Barack Obama a one-term president.

Heritage Foundation
This organization is considered the Republican think tank; located on Capitol Hill (in Washington D.C.) and is run by former-Senator *Jim DeMint* (SC). Its stated mission: *To formulate and promote conservative public policies based on the principles of free enterprise, limited government, individual freedom, traditional American values, and a strong national defense.* The group's political arm, *Heritage Action*, was instrumental in the 2013 government shutdown, warning Republican lawmakers who supported a compromise with the President that there would be consequences in the 2014 midterm elections. So much for that "individual freedom" thing.

U.S. Chamber of Commerce
Contrary to popular belief, this is not an agency of the U.S. government. On the contrary, it is the biggest lobbying group and represents the interests of many businesses and trade associations. It is staffed with policy specialists, lobbyists and lawyers; and does not disclose its donors.

America Rising
A GOP research Super PAC; run by GOP operatives with Mitt Romney's campaign manager, *Matt Rhoades* at the helm, supported by Republican National Committee aides *Joe Pounder* and *Tim Miller*. The group sends staffers to track Democratic candidates with the goal of capturing their gaffes. In addition, the researchers dig into histories of Democratic candidates searching for anything that can be used as dirt and smear. America Rising then shares information with their fellow conservatives.

FreedomWorks
Founded by billionaire brothers *Charles Koch* and *David Koch*, this group focuses on mobilizing rank-and-file Republicans to support the candidates running for office. Freedomworks creates the rank-and-file Republican supporters in boot camps where the grassroots activists learn Rightwing propaganda and how to intimidate and threaten any Republicans who break from the party's orthodoxy. Their key political issues include:

- Budget and Spending

- Health Care Reform
- Fundamental Tax Reform, Energy and the Environment
- Workplace Freedom
- School Choice
- Red Tape, Hidden Taxes, and Regulation
- Medicare, Social Security and Entitlement Reform

Club for Growth

Run by former Indiana Representative *Chris Chocola*, this group is a take-no-prisoners enforcer for Republican candidates who pledge to lower taxes (for the rich); and has sketched out a strategy to go after incumbent Republicans who stray from the group's line. The Club has two political arms: an affiliated traditional Political Action Committee called the *Club for Growth PAC* (endorses and raises money for fiscally conservative candidates) and *Club for Growth Action,* an independent-expenditure only committee or Super-PAC. The Club for Growth's policy goals include:

- cutting income tax rates
- repealing the estate tax
- limited government
- balanced budget amendment
- entitlement reform
- free trade
- tort reform
- school choice
- deregulation

Senate Conservatives Fund

In the tradition of the Heritage Foundation and FreedomWorks, and aligned with the Tea Party, this political action committee, founded by former-Senator *Jim DeMint* (SC), promises to politically punish compromise-minded Republicans. In other words, they support gridlock in Congress by refusing to compromise with Democrats on any bills they try to pass. But at the same time, they expect Democrats to support Republican bills. The Senate Conservatives Fund political goals include:

- smaller government
- abolish the IRS
- repeal Obamacare

There you have it! The behind the scenes of the Republican Party!
So, whatever Rightwing issues that pops up in the news, you can
now figure out who is really behind it. But how do they get the
word out to their masses of minions?

Fox News

I first watched Fox News by shear accident. I was channel-surfing
one day to get the latest on what's going on with the 2008 Obama
campaign. I arbitrarily stopped on Fox. I heard some bad news at
first, or so I thought. But as I continued to listen, it became
obvious these people had personal issues with Barack Obama. It
didn't seem like news anymore as much as *"We really, really,
really, really, really hate this guy!"* For a little while, I gave them
the benefit of doubt. I then thought, *"Oh, this is a rightwing
station and they're bashing a Democratic candidate."* But there is
bashing a person because he's a Democrat and there is bashing a
person because of the color of his skin. The more I watched Fox
News, the more the later seemed more apparent.

Is Fox News a racist network? I've been asking myself that
question and trying to find a definite answer. Although, it might
seem they are because they have yet to say anything positive
about President Obama, they can claim it's only because he is a
Democrat. But does any other network that claims to be "news"
have such a questionable reputation? In addition, does any other
network that claims to be "news" have so many challenges to that
claim? For instance, there are those who claim Fox News is more
entertainment; not news. And there are those who claim Fox News
only promotes a rightwing perspective; not unbiased journalism.
And there are those who claim, Fox News is fake news; not
responsible news journalism. And finally, there are those who
claim Fox News is nothing more than comedy, like the Daily Show
or Saturday Night Live. It appears, the loyal Fox News viewers are
the only ones who take Fox News serious!

During the time I watched Fox News Channel, I noticed an obvious
overdose of "personal opinions" being passed off as facts. Dare I
add to the list, Fox News is *"opinionated views"*, not news? Not
entirely! According to Fox News, its daily news hours are *"9am to*

4pm" and *"6pm to 8pm"* for a total of 9 news hours a day. In other words, *"The O'Reilly Factor (4am to 5am)",* is not news! In other words, *"Hannity (5am to 6am)",* is not news! In other words, *"Fox and Friends (6am to 9am)",* is not news! In other words, Fox has 15-hours of programming that includes its most popular shows they themselves do not consider news but rather opiniontainment! However, the opinionate-hosts at Fox might very well influence the new stories. For instance, a subject (i.e. *Is President Obama really a Muslim?*) is passed from one opinion-host to the next. By the time you get to the actual news, they headline, *"Some Americans are wondering if President Obama is really a Muslim."* But those *"some Americans"* are really the opinionated hosts at Fox News.

The Numero Uno shareholder of Fox News is *Keith Rupert Murdoch*, an Australian-American tabloid mogul. In the 1950s and '60s, he acquired various newspapers in Australia and New Zealand. In 1969, he expanded to the United Kingdom, taking over the *News of the World,* followed closely by *The Sun*. In 1974, he moved to New York to expand into the U.S. market. In 1981, he bought his first British broadsheet, *The Times*. And in 1985, his *News Corporation* acquired *Twentieth Century Fox*. This was also the year he became a naturalized U.S. citizen. In 1989, his global media holding company the *News Corporation* acquired *HarperCollins*, one of the world's leading English-language publishers. And in 2007, he added *The Wall Street Journal* to his media empire collection. I had no idea the Journal was technically foreign-owned, now.

These are but a few of the more notable companies the Murdoch empire owns. By the year 2000, News Corporation owned over 800 companies in more than 50 countries with a net worth of over $5-billion. According to the 2011 list of Forbes richest Americans, Rupert Murdoch is the 38th richest person in the U.S. and the 106th-richest person in the world, with a net worth of $8.3 billion. Now, you can see his shareholdership in Fox News is really small potatoes; he dam near owns half the media on the planet! OK, that just might have been a bit of an exaggeration. But not when you consider he has been listed three times in the *Time 100* among the most influential people in the world. And in May 2012, *Forbes* ranked him as the 24th most powerful person on the planet. Fox News Channel was launched in October 1996. Rupert Murdoch asked former U.S. Republican Party political strategist *Roger Ailes* to start it. Is it a stretch to suggest Fox News is an extension of Roger Ailes' rightwing views?

Does any other organization that claims to be "news" have such a hard time trying to make millions of people accept it as news? Perhaps, this has something to do with the fact, Fox News blatantly promotes exclusive Rightwing propaganda, terminology, myths and hoaxes. Hence, most (if not all) of what Fox News promotes is fictional, imaginary, and does not exist in the real world.

Fox News Hoaxes (i)

Media Matters for America (a progressive research and information center, monitors, analyzes, and corrects Rightwing misinformation in the U.S. media), listed what it called the ten most *"egregious examples"* of *"distortion"* by Fox News. The criticism includes several examples of cropping quotes from President Obama so they appear out-of-context, using image-manipulation software to edit the appearance of reporters from *The New York Times* and using footage from other events during a report on the November 5 Tea Party rally in Washington, DC to make it appear as if a larger number of protesters attended the event.

In September 2009, the Obama administration engaged in a verbal conflict with Fox News Channel. As a result, President Obama appeared on all major news programs except Fox News. They were ignored by the president, because of unflattering remarks about the president made by Fox News commentators Glenn Beck and Sean Hannity, and Fox coverage of Obama's health-care proposal. In addition, White House officials referred to Fox News Channel as *"not a news network"*. *Anita Dunn* (White House Communications Director) added, *"Fox News often operates as either the research arm or the communications arm of the Republican Party"*. Fox News has a tendency to insult people then play the victim when the people they insulted retaliate. In this case, the Fox News spin on this incident was, *"The White House War On Fox!"*, as though Fox News didn't start the war with the White House with all of its negative and unfounded news reports.

My own personal observations of Fox News begins with the terminology it uses; they redefine a lot of words that they build their rhetoric around. For instance ...

There is no such thing as a "Liberal"

The word *"liberal"* is an adjective; a word that describes a noun. There can be a person with "liberal ideas" or with "liberal views" but those are in contrast to conservative ideals and views. Fox News labels everyone who challenges the Rightwing propaganda they promote, a "Liberal" or "Liberals". In this regard, "Liberal" is a derogatory name directed at people Fox News disenfranchises in one form or another.

There is no such thing as a "Leftwinger"

There are politics in general that serve the vast majority of the people; based on the U.S. Constitution and there are *"Rightwing politics"* that exclusively serve the rich minority, their private corporations and contradict the U.S. Constitution! However, Fox News (the Rightwing propaganda machine) is an organization that excels in *"derogatory name-calling"*. They just don't expect anyone to realize that is what they do! In this particular case, any ideal, comment, suggestion, or policy that contradicts or challenges the Rightwing politics that Fox News endorses are labeled with their derogatory name, *"Leftwing"*. What exactly do they mean by it? The contempt and very nasty undertone that accompanies this expression suggests, they don't mean anything good when using it. In addition, Fox News labels the people who support such ideas, *Leftwingers* or *Leftists*. Whether they consider themselves this or not, Fox News and it's viewers never ask! Instead, they instantly regurgitate (and label you with) these derogatory names.

There's no such thing as "The Liberal Media"

According to *Media Matters for America* (the progressive research and information center committed to monitoring, analyzing, and correcting Rightwing misinformation in the media), as well as, plain observation, Fox News stories are invented with:

- strategically (deceitfully) edited video clips
- news articles with strategic deletions
- comments quoted out-of-context
- distorted details and misinformation

- archived video footage to pass off as current events
- re-defined words (e.g. socialism, marriage, liberal)
- polls taken with faulty input to manipulate the outcome
- survey data from 25 to 50 year old polls pretending its current
- eradicating all Republican involvement
- people lying through their teeth

Then they label all the legitimate, rational, and responsible news organizations that contradicts Fox News distortions, *"The Liberal Mainstream Media"*. This is so the gullible Fox News viewers will think everyone else is lying and Fox News is the only one telling them the truth! In psychology, this is no different than a person claiming, *"Everyone is crazy, except me!"*

There's no such thing as a "Liberal Agenda"
I have heard this expression time and time again on Fox News and by Rightwing minions. But not once have I ever heard anyone explain exactly what this *"Liberal Agenda"* is, or what they mean by it. But I would imagine his is yet another derogatory expression invented by Rightwing advocates to suggest something is a serious, or damaging threat ... to their Rightwing policies. I read online on a rightwing website that asked and answered, *"What is the Far-Left Liberal Agenda? Liberalism is for Government Takeover and the Removal of Your Freedoms!"* My observation is the fact Rightwing propaganda is based on contradictions! The word *"liberal"* is one of several words based on the Latin root *"liber"* which means *"free"* as expressed in words from the same root, "liberate" and "liberty". So, when Rightwing advocates suggest anything involving the Latin root "liber" has anything to do with the opposite of "free", they are contradicting themselves with propaganda they invented.

There's no such thing as "Liberal Biased"
For once, the word "Liberal" is used in its proper context as an adjective. Be that as it may, is it being properly used in this term? The word *"liberal"* means: *free from bigotry and prejudice*. On the other hand, the word *"biased"* means (and is synonymous with): *bigotry and prejudice*. So, how can Rightwing advocates claim an idea is "free" from bigotry and prejudice while at the same time claiming it includes bigotry and prejudice? As previously stated, Rightwing propaganda is saturated with contradictions. In addition to that, Rightwing advocates always use this term to the extent of

name-calling. They never reveal the contrasting idea to the idea they label "liberal biased". Why? Because that contrasting idea is the one that is actually biased between the two.

There's no such thing as "The Other Side Of The Story"
Fox News often claims it provides "the other side of the story". This is the first indication the Fox News version of the story will be different than what every other news organization is reporting (which is the same story). In reality, there is no such thing as "the other side of a news story". There is just *"the news story"* and the facts it entails! Fox News invents a distorted version of the story via a series of the aforementioned tactics, then calls it "the other side" of what everyone else is reporting. But how could it be "the other side" when Fox News' version was invented by deleting up to one-half of the facts? Typically, this means editing out any Republican involvement to give the impression only President Obama and/or the White House was involved.

Fair and Balanced News, Seriously?
Begin by realizing, *"Fair and Balanced"* is Fox News' opinion of itself. No one else calls them that! Journalists realize this is not a slogan as much as it is a disclaimer. Fox News is announcing (for legal reasons) it is about to broadcast fabricated, exaggerated, sensationalized, and tabloid-like stories! In Tabloid Journalism, the expression, "Fair and Balanced", means: "Lies mixed with Truth" in order to produce a "fair and balanced (lies mixed-in with truth)" report! The expression has nothing to do with reporting accurate news stories. But Fox News has never taken the time to explain this little tidbit to its viewers. Instead, Fox News misleads them into thinking what they are about to hear is the most factual interpretation of events they will ever get!

We Report, You Decide?
I've listened to Fox News reports and the only thing I decided was the fact Fox News leads it's viewers into making a pre-determined decision; or drawing the conclusion Fox News wants them to draw. Fox News does not make a direct statement. Instead, they make insinuates all day long until Fox News viewers decide the insinuations they've been hearing all day are factual statements. This way, Fox News can always deny they said a particular thing if it ever comes back to haunt them.

We're #1 In Cable News!

Once again, this is Fox News' opinion of itself. None of the other networks make this claim! The truth of the matter is Fox News only leads in what The Nielsen Ratings call, *"The Average Talley (Rating)"*. Fox News viewers are instructed in the FreedomWorks boot camp to leave their TVs tuned-in on Fox News Channel, lingering on it all day long. This way each viewer is counted *"multiple times"* in Nielsen's average rating! Hence, Fox News is #1 (in Nielsen's average rating) because they cheat! The opposite happens with the other cable news organizations where viewers tune-in just long enough to get the news then change the channel.

Every news organization knows Fox News "trails" all other cable stations in the more accurate *"Cumulative Ratings"* that give the same weight to the "*Light Viewer* (who tunes in for a brief time)" as it does the "*Heavy Viewer* (who lingers on a channel all day)". Unfortunately, the Rightwing minions get away with quoting the distorted Average Talley rating online and on TV, making it appear like the only data available.

Fox News Hoaxes (ii)

Often I would hear either Fox News or Rightwing advocates talk about issues out-of-context or in a sense that suggests they don't fully understand what it is they are commenting on. For instance, they would talk about the national debt as though it is a $17-trillion mortgage that the taxpayers make monthly payments on. Let me take some time to explain this, and other concepts, in full detail.

The Looming National Debt Myth

The *national debt* (a.k.a. public debt; government debt) is the amount of debt owed by the federal government; accumulated from having to finance government operations and divided into two categories: marketable securities and non-marketable securities. The government borrows in the sense of issuing/selling marketable securities (i.e. treasury notes, bills, and bonds) to individuals, businesses and other countries (governments), globally. The non-marketable securities represent amounts owed to program beneficiaries, such as, the Social Security Trust Fund, the Federal Housing Administration, the Federal Savings and Loan Corporation's

Resolution Fund and the Federal Hospital Insurance Trust Fund (Medicare). The measure of the national debt is the value of the <u>marketable securities</u> still outstanding at that point of time.

In essence, the national debt is not "debt" in the sense of owing a large balance on a loan. On the contrary, it consists of government bonds, bills and treasury notes the federal government sold to individuals, groups, businesses and countries to generate income to fund enormously expensive projects! For example, when George W. Bush had two wars and tax cuts to finance, the federal government sold billions of dollars worth of U.S. securities to the People's Republic of China to finance Bush's tax and war efforts. These (and all other) securities have *"maturity dates"* set for 25-years after the date of purchase. Hence, only those securities that mature(d) in 2013 got paid "with interest". And the securities set to mature in 2014 will be paid in 2014 "with interest".

Now, the *Gross Domestic Product* (GDP) is a measure of the total size and output of the U.S. economy on an annual basis. One of the most common ways to measure the severity of the national debt is to compare it to the GDP (i.e. the debt-to-GDP ratio). Mathematically speaking, this is the national debt amount divided by the GDP amount. Ideally, a low debt-to-GDP ratio indicates an economy that produces and sells goods and services sufficient to pay back debts without incurring further debt. And of course, the higher the debt-to-GDP, the worse off we are. Now, let's examine the debt-to-GDP ratio during the George W. Bush administration:

2001 = 55.9%   [George W. Bush]
2002 = 57.3%
2003 = 59.5%
2004 = 61.3%
2005 = 62.7%
2006 = 63.3%
2007 = 63.9%
2008 = 64.8%

Let's continue the debt-to-GDP trek during the succeeding Obama administration. And remember, he entered the White House in the midst of a collapsing economy indicated by the previous rising debt-to-GDP from the previous administration:

2009 = 76%   [Barack H. Obama]
2010 = 87.1%
2011 = 95.2%
2012 = 99.4%
2013 = **101.6%**

Rightwing advocates refuse to acknowledge the fact the U.S. economy did not slam on breaks when George W. Bush left the White House, reset, and start from zero when Barack H. Obama entered the White House.   The momentum from the previous administration kept on going into the succeeding administration. And as alarming as this final debt-to-GDP ratio might look, this is not the worst situation the U.S. has ever been in.   Consider the debt-to-GDP ratio before and after World War II:

1942 = 50.2%   [Franklin D. Roosevelt]
1943 = 54.9%
1944 = 79.1%
1945 = 97.6%   [Harry S. Truman]   [World War II ended]
1946 = **117.5%**
1947 = **121.7%**
1948 = **110.3%**
1949 = 98.2%
1950 = 93.1%
1960 = 58.6%   [Dwight D. Eisenhower]
1970 = 36.7%   [Richard M. Nixon]
1980 = 31.8%   [Jimmy Carter]

I am not suggesting these presidents were bad at their jobs, as much as, the country had much worse to deal with in regards to the national debt/GDP ratio, and survived.   And from what we can tell from the Truman administration, the ratio will get worse before it can get better!   Now, let's take a look at the debt-to-GDP ratio during the Reagan administration:

1981 = 31.9%   [Ronald Reagan]
1982 = 32.2%
1983 = 36.1%

1984 = 38.3%
1985 = 41.2%
1986 = 45.1%
1987 = 48.7%
1988 = 49.8%

Now, let's continue through the George H.W. Bush administration:

1989 = 51.1%   [George H.W. Bush]
1990 = 52.9%
1991 = 57.6%
1992 = 62.4%

So, if Rightwing advocates want to criticize economies during particular administrations, between Ronald Reagan and George H.W. Bush, the national debt/GDP ratio went from 31.9% to 62.4%. It nearly doubled! Now, let's take a look during the Bill Clinton administration:

1993 = 64.3%   [Bill Clinton]
1994 = 66.6%
1995 = 66.2%
1996 = 66.1%
1997 = 66.3%
1998 = 64.7%
1999 = 62.2%
2000 = 60.1%

Now, you can go back and put the ratios during the George W. Bush administration in their proper perspective; it began running on momentum from the previous Clinton administration but ended worse than it began. And this worse momentum that ended the George W. Bush administration trickled into the following Obama administration. Be that as it may, Rightwing advocates continue to focus on the actual dollar amount of the national debt and blowing it completely out of proportion. Although we have the highest national debt in U.S. history, we do not have the highest national debt-to-GDP ratio. And once again, the national debt-to-GDP ratio is a more accurate indicator of damaging debt than the actual amount of debt. Think of your own debt situation. You compare your total debt to your total income to stay on the safe side.

Fox News Hoaxes (iii)

Actually, I did not think the national debt would take up the entire previous chapter. So, here's "Part 3" of examining the hoaxes Fox News invents and tries to pass off as factual information!

Obama is a Muslim?

One of the first assaults from the Right caught me completely by surprise, *"Barack Obama is a Muslim!"* What? He is? Shocking! And then I caught myself. Hey, wait a minute! Do I really care? I really didn't know that much about Barack Obama's personal life. I was one to find things out for myself then make up my own mind; not let outside sources tell me, influence me, or bully me into thinking what THEY want me to think. So that's what I did. I started exploring this new guy, Barack Obama. Was he a Muslim? Were the people making these accusations even "Christians" or were they simply bigots spewing their hatred for Muslims?

I must admit, if Barack Obama did anything, it was bring the bigots out in force. I just happened to hear him address the Muslim issue on some TV spot. He admitted, he is a Christian. He continued to announce the church he and his family attended. Hmmm. That was enough for me! But what did surprise me was the fact those people from the extreme Right kept insisting he is a Muslim. As though being a Muslim is worse than being a bigot. I concluded, if they don't put forth any effort to prove THEY are even Christians, I won't accept their accusation, Barack Obama is a Muslim!

Some of the Rightwing minions called him a "secret Muslim" or a "closet Muslim" or a "Muslim in denial." They kept on insisting Barack Obama is a Muslim. Eventually, the nasty undertone they attached to the word "Muslim" started to sound more like code for "nigger." And if this were the case, it started to make perfect sense. Oh. So, now I have to try to read between the lines when the extreme Right makes a silly accusation about the black guy running for President. This forced me to start paying closer attention to everything that came from the Right. And whatever they said, I researched the hell out of it. This approach is what led to my Black belt in politics! Or at least, understanding the Right.

Does the extreme Right use the word "Muslim" to cover up what they truly want to say? Do they ever claim they themselves are Christians or do they expect you will assume it? All they say is, *"Barack Obama is a Muslim!"* Thus, you're suppose to assume they are Christians. That's the extent of it! Now, what exactly do they mean? The man admitted on national TV he practices Christianity. How can these Rightwing extremists insist he is a Muslim based on nothing more than their own biased and irrational opinion? Well. Perhaps, *"Muslim"* is really code for something else.

I've heard the Rightwing argument, he is not a Christian! But this is basically indirectly calling him a Muslim. Now, what do they mean by *"Christian"*? On the other side of the planet, Europeans are called "Christians" by Muslims. This does not refer to religion, per say. To them, *"Christian"* is a euphemism for European. In this same regard, Europeans us the word *"Muslim"* to refer to the dark-skinned Arabs they use to call, Moors. It was beginning to sound as though the extreme Right was using this same thought process. Instead of expressing their true feelings, they use code. Hence, *"Muslim = Nigger"* and *"Christian = Rightwing extremist"*. The statement, *"Barack Obama is not a Christian, he is a Muslim!"* really means, *"Barack Obama is not white, he is a nigger!"*

Right advocates seem to think they are more clever than the rest of us! They think, no one will ever notice all the nasty undertones associated with certain words in the terminology they use.

The N-Word Myth
One thing I noticed about the extreme Right, they are not big on knowing the whole story. They cling to carefully selected details that support the desired conclusion and ignore the rest. Whatever they say, I investigate further to get all the details they leave out.

I came to find out when white bigots use the n-word, it literally shows complete stupidity. The main reason being, the n-word evolved out of complete stupidity! And after you know the story behind the n-word, you will never ever consider using it (or think it) again and the taboo associated with the n-word will magically disappear. And if you ever hear anyone using the n-word, you will realize how stupid they are. But bear in mind, this has nothing to do with Black people (or people of any color, these days) calling each other, "Niggas".

In the mid-1600s, about 40% of African laborers (a.k.a. slaves) were imported from the west African coast of Niger (NAHY-jer). The other 60% of African laborers were smaller groups who came from several other areas up and down the west African coast line. Regardless, they all eventually wound up in the same spot; the auction blocks in the state of Virginia. Be that as it may, the hillbillies and rednecks at the time were not the most educated bunch. Most of the common folks had no formal education at all. Therefore, it was a common thing when adults did not know how to read. Most of those who did, read with not more than a 2nd or 3rd grade level. While selling the human cargo, information was verbally disclosed to all potential buyers. This included where the cargo originated.

As the auctioneers did their verbal best to make the human cargo sound more desirable to buyers, they included in their sales pitch some of the mysterious places the cargo came from: Ethiopia, the Congo, Ghana and ... "Ni"-"ger". As previously stated, most of the cargo originated from the African country of Niger (NAHY-jer). Since the erroneously pronounced "Nigger" was their homeland, most African laborers were called, Niggers. Often time, "Nigger" was used as a prefix attached to the first name to identify where the cargo originated. For example, an African slave given the name, Charlie, was called, Nigger-Charlie; an African slave given the name, George, was called, Nigger-George. This instantly differentiated them from any of the whites using the same name.

The Ethiops were recognized in the same way but "Nigger" rolled off the tongue a lot easier. It became the moniker of all Africans. Also, there were more Niggers than Ethiops, Ghanas or Congos. Now, remember at this point the word Nigger was not used in a derogatory manner; mean-spirited and nasty undertones were not associated with it. The word "Nigger" merely acknowledged the homeland where the African slaves came from. It was not different than distinguishing Joe from Alabama and Joe from Tennessee. Taking it one step further, if a black was known by a particular trade, like Blacksmith, he would be called, the Nigger Blacksmith.

Bear in mind, this all evolved from the fact white auctioneers did not know the word "Niger" was French. So upon seeing it, they instantly applied basic English grammar pronouncing it, "ni"-"ger"; with no hostile intent behind it. Just a simple mispronunciation! Now, here's a bit of trivia: In the late 1890s, the coastal area was severed from inland Niger and renamed "Nigeria" by the British empire. This was also not common knowledge among the folks of Virginia. But had it been, it would've mattered very little. The Nigger mentality was already deeply rooted in the southern States. This also explains how it became deeply embedded in blacks, using Ebonics, to call each other a variation of the same word. If a bunch of non-English speaking Africans were told they came from "ni"-"ger" while learning to speak English, that's what they began calling each other. A tradition that still exists today!

With this in mind, do white bigots get to define every black person on the face of the planet? Intelligent people know the word Nigger means you came from the African country of Niger/Nigeria. In reality, less than 1% of all black people come from the African country of Niger/Nigeria. To suggest the other 99%(+) come from the same country only reflects the same stupidity as those who mispronounced the word in the first place, over 400-years ago. As a matter of fact, many of us still do this same thing today with countries like Iraq, Iran and Pakistan. It's not EYE-ROCK, EYE-RAN and PACK-ish-stan; it's IR-rock, IR-rahn and PAHK-eesh-ston. Some say, EYE-talian (Italian) and AYE-rab (Arab) when it's eh-TAL-ian and AIR-rahb.

Are all Asian people Chinese? Call a person from Korean, Japan or Vietnam, "Chinese," they will be offended. Not because they hate Chinese, as much as, YOU are so stupid! Are all Latinos from Mexico? Call a Cuban, Puerto Rican or Panamanian, "Mexican", and they will be offended. Not because they hate Mexicans but rather because YOU are so stupid! With this in mind, if you don't have anything personal against people from Niger/Nigeria don't call black people not from that country the n-word. That is, unless you are just plain stuck on your own stupidity.

And by the way, President Obama's ancestry is Kenyan.

Blacks Call Each Other the N-Word?

It confuses a lot of white people when they hear black people using the n-word among themselves knowing they would be offended if white people called them the n-word. This is a legitimate concern and understandably so. Let's get to the bottom of this great mystery before we go any further! We already know what white bigots in the south meant when they used the n-word in the 1800s during slavery versus when they used it in the 1900s long after slavery was over and done with.

When white bigots of the 20th century used the n-word, they meant nothing good by it. The n-word carried all the jealousy, envy, hate and resentment white bigots felt towards black people. Why did they feel this way? Did I mention jealousy, envy, hate and resentment? It was really nothing any blacks had done towards whites in the south. Wait a minute! Maybe that Civil War thing had something to do with it. As history dictates, at a certain point it was obvious the war was not going good for the northern Union army. But the tables were suddenly, magically and mysteriously turned on the southern Confederacy. The only detail I can find to explain this shift in power was from adding black Union soldiers to the battlefield. Now, I'm open to any other reason(s) you might come up with. But this reason to me is clear, for now.

After the Confederacy collapsed, I can see the white bigots in the south blaming it all on the blacks who fought for the north; who turned the tides of the war as the south lost everything. But as bigots would have it, they always take the simple route. Instead of confining the blame to the blacks who actually fought in the war, they directed their resentment towards all black people. Thus, they direct their 20th century version of the n-word to all black people. But the n-word evolved in a different timeline among black people. In the 19th century, both blacks and whites used the word "Nigger" for the same reasons; none of which were derogatory. But among blacks, the n-word evolved into a euphemism to describe several different sentiments.

Allow me to specify, not all African-Americans speak Ebonics, but those who do use the n-word in a variety of ways. For instance:

- best friend - (Kevin iz mah nigga!);
- friendly acquaintances - (What's up mah nigga?);
- I'm madly in-love with you - (you MAH nigga!);
- complete stranger - (Hey, see dat nigga over dare?);
- I disagree with your dumbass - (ni@@a Pleeez!!!);
- the best in his field - (He is one bad-ass nigga!);

Now, can you see the different paths of evolution the n-word has taken among southern white ex-Confederate bigots and among southern black former-slaves? By now, many of those southerners, both black and white, have relocated to northern states and they took their traditions with them.

It's Obama's Fault, Seriously?

Since Barack Obama's inauguration, the Rightwing minions claim everything under the sun is Obama's fault! For instance, according to the Bureau of Labor Statistics' database, when George W. Bush left the White House the national unemployment rate was 7.8%. One month after President Obama's inauguration, it rose to 8.3%. The Rightwing minions claim this is the result of Barack Obama moving into the White House. By late 2001, unemployment rose as high as 10.6%. Be that as it may, was this the result of anything President Obama had done or was it still the upward momentum?

The Rightwing minions seem to think things that affect the economy happen overnight. On the contrary, the unemployment rate today is not the result of decisions people made yesterday but rather the result of decisions people made months ago! For example, when George W. Bush was inaugurated in 2001, he inherited a national unemployment rate of 3.9% from the previous Bill Clinton administration (down from 4.1% in August). The rate fluctuated throughout most of Bush's two terms but in December 2007 into 2008, it began to climb higher and higher and higher. Here's a snapshot of the rising unemployment rate according to the Bureau of Labor Statistics (as of this writing):

January 2001, **4.2%**
January 2008, **5.0%**
May 2008, **5.4%**

August 2008, **6.1**%
November 2008, **6.8**%
December 2008, **7.3**%
January 2009 (Obama's inauguration), **7.8**%
February 2009 (Obama's first full month in office), **8.3**%
March 2009, **8.7**%
April 2009, **9.0**%
May 2009, **9.4**%
June 2009, **9.5**%
August 2009, **9.6**%
September 2009, **9.8**%
October 2009, **10.0**%

As you can now clearly see, the national unemployment numbers during the Obama administration are not indicative to Barack Obama's time in office. On the contrary, they are continued momentum from the previous George W. Bush administration. Like the national debt, the unemployment rate did not slam on breaks when George W. Bush left the White House, reset and start up again after Barack Obama's inauguration.

However, when the numbers did slam on breaks and do a complete 180°, you can attribute that as indicative to the actions of the Obama administration. In November 2009, the unemployment rate began to decline to what it is today. Here's a snapshot:

October 2009, **10.0**% (Slammed on breaks!)
November 2009, **9.9**% (Start declining)
January 2010, **9.7**%
May 2010, **9.6**%
July 2010, **9.5**%
November 2010, **9.8**% (Midterm Elections)
December 2010, **9.4**%
January 2011, **9.1**%
February 2011, **9.0**%
October 2011, **8.8**%
November 2011, **8.6**%
December 2011, **8.5**%
January 2012, **8.2**%
August 2012, **8.1**%
September 2012, **7.8**%

February 2013, **7.7**%
March 2013, **7.5**%
July 2013, **7.3**%
November 2013, **7.0**%
December 2013, **6.7**%
January 2014, **6.6**%

Using their same logic, the Rightwing minions try to take the credit for the decline in unemployment by claiming it was 9.8% in November 2010 and the very next month it dropped to 9.4, and has been declining ever since! On the contrary, the more rational explanation, unemployment had been declining from 10.0% in October 2009 to 9.5% in July 2010 (stagnate through October). It then hit a snafu in November 2010 (jumping back up to 9.8%), then resumed its downward descent of 9.4% in December 2010. Personally, I would not put it past Republicans to get the private corporations they represent to *"temporarily freeze hiring practices"* (or something) to show a fake-inflated unemployment rate of 9.8% during the November 2010 midterm elections. But that's just me!

Theoretically speaking, if Republicans had anything to do with the declining unemployment rate, they had to do something to make it happen. What exactly did they do? Since Republicans took control of the House of Representatives, they've done anything BUT create jobs. To name a few, they:

- voted to repeal President Obama's healthcare reform;
- attempted to de-fund Global Warming (climate change) research;
- attempted to defund healthcare;
- proposed a budget to cut billions of dollars in aid to the poor, the homeless, women and children;
- extended the Patriot Act;
- attempted to cut funding for Planned Parenthood and PBS;
- attempted to "redefine rape" to no longer include statutory rape, incest rape, or spousal rape (all of which are what Republican politicians often get convicted for).
- cut Pell grants;
- attempted to cut $1-billion from Head Start; over 200,000 kids would lose their spots in preschool;
- worked to add guidelines to delay implementation of Don't Ask, Don't Tell repeal, despite overwhelming support for its repeal;

- proposed policy to allow a hospitalized pregnant woman to die instead of have a life saving abortion, if she needed it;
- attempted to cut money to Veterans;
- <u>voted to fund</u> chemical contraception for wild horses; <u>voted to cut funding</u> for contraception for human women;
- voted to continue spending millions of tax payer dollars to sponsor a NASCAR racecar;
- voted against letting the last surviving, American WWI veteran be honored in the Capitol building's rotunda, after he passed away;
- continue to support the George W. Bush policies that lost jobs;

Any rational person can see, since Republicans took control of the House, none of their activity has attributed to job creation. Suggesting the economy improved from a dominant Republican presence, is completely delusional. Whatever President Obama had been doing has been working. And the truth of the matter is, most of the Dixiecrats who worked against the President were not re-elected in the 2010 midterm election. Unfortunately, this meant Republicans had to replace them. Perhaps, the lesser of two evils?

The Need For Speed

In an effort to deny President Obama any credit for the declining unemployment numbers, the Rightwing minions started quoting inflated rates from a website called, Portal Seven. Among other things, this is a database that provides statistics on unemployment in Europe, the United States and Japan. I compared the portal seven unemployment rates to those listed at the Bureau of Labor Statistics (bls.gov) and started making comparisons. For starts, the BLS website is a **.gov** (provided by independent agency, General Services Administration) website and Portal Seven website is a **.com** (commercial business) website. Instantly, the two sites have a difference in intentions.

I searched around on Alexa.com, a website that provides statistics on other websites, and discovered, 45.9% of Portal Seven's audience comes from India, 7.2% is from the Philippines and 6.4%, the United States. In contrast, 71% of BLS's audience comes from the United States and 6.5% from India. I can't help but to wonder why does Portal Seven have so much traffic from India? Then again, India is one of the first countries US businesses started outsourcing to. In more detail, Portal Seven is visited mostly by females between the ages of 25-34, have no children, graduate school educated and do their browsing from work. In comparison, BLS is mostly visited by females between the ages of 55-64, received some college education and browse from school.

At this point, I'm not really sure of Portal Seven's intended target audience but it sure has caught the attention of the female mid-adult population of India. However, the Portal Seven audience also consists of 6.4% in the United States. Who are these people? So far it seems they are the Rightwing minions looking for ways to inflate the unemployment rates. Portal Seven provides the official unemployment rates one can find at the BLS. But it also provides inflated unemployment rates based on other criteria. There are six categories of unemployment rates one can explore:

U-1 - percentages of unemployed 15-weeks or longer
U-2 - percentages of labor force who lost jobs or completed temporary assignments.
U-3 - the official unemployment rate per the International Labor Organization (United Nations) definition
U-4 - the U-3 level plus discouraged workers who stopped looking This level continues to suggest the U-4s stopped looking for work; current economic conditions make them believe no work is available. But I'm not convinced they took a survey versus expressed an unfounded opinion.
U-5 - the U-4 level plus marginally attached workers, loosely attached workers or those who "would like" and are able to work but have not looked for work recently.
U-6 – the U-5 level plus part-time workers who want to work full time but cannot due to economic reasons.

Hey, why not add a U-7 level consisting of retired people deceased people, and hospitalized people? Anyway, the Rightwing minions for some reason quote from the U6 level of Portal Seven. The rates listed are at least double the official BLS rate. Hence, instead of accepting the BLS's reported 7% unemployment rate, the Rightwing minions quote the U6 rate of 14%, instead. I would take them serious if it were not for the fact, they quote the BLS rates for George W. Bush's time in the White House.

One Term President?

In February 2009, just 10-days after his inauguration, President Obama did an interview with NBC's Matt Lauer. While talking about bailing out banks, Laurer asked the President, *"At some point will you say, 'Wait a minute, we've spent this amount of money, we're not seeing the results, we've got to change course dramatically?'"* President Obama: *"Look, I'm at the start of my administration. One nice thing about the situation I find myself in is that – I will be held accountable. I've got 4-years. And ... you know, a year from now, I think people are going to see that we're starting to make some progress but there's still gonna be some pain out there. <u>If I don't have this done in 3-years, then there's going to be a one-term proposition</u>."*

From that point forward, the Rightwing minions were running around claiming President Obama said, *"If I don't fix the economy in 3-years, I will be a one-term president."* When the Rightwing minions get a piece of gossip about President Obama, they're like a junkyard dog with a bone; they won't let it go. They keep repeating the rumor among themselves, until they believe the rumor is factual information. Another variation of the same rumor, *"If I don't fix the national debt in 3-years, I will be a one-term president."* As usual, Rightwing minions wait to be told what to think; either via the FreedomWorks boot camp or FOX NEWS. But their rhetoric consists of nothing more than rumors and innuendo.

In its proper context, Matt Lauer and President Obama were taking about the *Troubled Asset Relief Program (TARP)* and whether its economic benefits would merit the costs ($700-billion). Hence, Laurer's question, *"At some point will you say, 'Wait a minute, we've spent this amount of money, we're not seeing the results, we've got to change course dramatically?'"* And President Obama's reply, *"Look, I'm at the start of my administration. One nice thing about the situation I find myself in is that – I will be held accountable. I've got 4-years. And ... you know, a year from now, I think people are going to see that we're starting to make some progress but there's still gonna be some pain out there. <u>If I don't have this (TARP) done in 3-years, then there's going to be a one-term proposition</u>."*

In case you who don't know, TARP is a program that allows the U.S. government to purchase assets and equity from financial institutions in an attempt to strengthen the financial sector. The TARP bill was signed into law by George W. Bush in October 2008 as a component to address the subprime mortgage crisis. Hence, provided infusions of capital to struggling banks, boosted Federal Reserve lending and launched a public-private effort to soften the blow of failed assets weighing on banks' books. But according to the *Government Accountability Office* (GOA), the lifetime cost of TARP was a mere $70-billion; just one-tenth of the amount first allocated by Congress. The TARP program also included financing for the auto industry, which has since experienced enough of a recovery to create more jobs and new profitability.

Among everything President Obama said in this interview was (and has repeated many times since), "*There's no silver bullets for the economy and it's going to take some time for us to be able to dig ourselves out of this hole.*"

Now, what exactly did President Obama mean when he used the phrase, "*one-term proposition*"? Was he referring to his presidency or was he referring to the amount of time it would take TARP to do what it was designed to do? Well, since the topic was TARP, and not the length of Obama's presidency, there is a very good chance the president was, in essence, saying, "*If TARP doesn't do what it was designed to do (during the first 3-years of my administration), then it's going to take one-term (4-years).*" Regardless to this fact, the Rightwing minions (in-charge of propaganda) excel in twisting, distorting and misrepresentation and they did not hesitate to twist, distort, misrepresent and quote out-of-context.

During an exclusive interview (January 2010), ABC World News anchor, *Diane Sawyer*, asked President Obama, "*Ever in the middle of all that's coming did you think maybe one term is enough?*" President Obama replied, "*You know, I -- I would say that -- the one thing I'm clear about is that I'd rather be a really good one-term president than a mediocre two-term president.*" And ever since, the Rightwing minions were running around claiming President Obama said, "*I want to be a one-term president!*" But the really sad part is, the Rightwing minions immediately spread this rumor among themselves without ever once finding out if it's true or not. They just blindly accept it and repeat it, repetitively. Perhaps, so often until they think it's the indubitable truth!

During an interview with National Journal's *Major Garrett*, several days before the November 2010 midterm elections, Senate Minority Leader *Mitch McConnell* [R] of Kentucky said, "We need to be honest with the public. This election is about them, not us. And we need to treat this election as the first step in retaking the government. We need to say to everyone on Election Day, 'Those of you who helped make this a good day, you need to go out and help us finish the job'." After Garret asked, "What's the job?", McConnell replied, *"The single most important thing we want to achieve is for President Obama to be a one-term president."*

House Republican Vote No Clause

Dozens of polls throughout 2011 showed the American people overwhelmingly named "jobs" and the "economy" the top two issues facing our country. In addition, the polls showed the American people support immigration reform and increasing the minimum wage. Yet, House Republicans failed to pass a single job creation bill, failed to take a single step toward immigration reform, and refused to raise the minimum wage for millions of American workers. Instead, they passed bills that give tax breaks to big oil companies that outsource American jobs overseas; voted up to 46 times to repeal Obamacare; and manufactured crisis after crisis:

The Fast and Furious Hoax

On October 26, 2009, a teleconference was held at the Department of Justice in Washington, D.C. to discuss the U.S. strategy for combating Mexican drug cartels. Participating in the meeting were:

- Deputy Attorney General David W. Ogden
- Assistant Attorney General Lanny A. Breuer
- Acting ATF Director Kenneth Melson
- DEA Administrator Michele Leonhart
- Director of the FBI Robert Mueller
- Several top federal prosecutors in the Southwestern border states

The group decided on a strategy to "identify" and "eliminate" entire arms trafficking networks rather than low-level buyers; they did not suggest using the "*gunwalking tactic* (purposely allow licensed firearms dealers to sell weapons to illegal straw buyers, hoping to track the guns to Mexican drug cartel leaders and arrest them). But Phoenix ATF supervisors eventually did use the gunwalking tactic in an attempt to achieve their desired goals. The operation began on October 31, 2009.

In May 2011, Republican House Oversight Committee Chairman *Darrell Issa* and Iowa Republican Senator *Chuck Grassley* asked U.S. States Attorney *Eric Holder* for details about Operation Fast and Furious and to turn over subpoenaed records. Holder counter-offered to provide the documents on the condition that doing so would satisfy the House Oversight Committee's subpoenas, resolve the dispute, and dispel the notion they were looking to "blame him" for an operation he was not directly involved in. After Holder called Republicans out on their witch hunt, they got mad and made a big stink about it, blowing everything out of proportion and twisting the facts on Fox News.

The Benghazi Hoax

On September 11, 2012, the American embassy in Benghazi, Libya was attacked and three Americans were killed. In the midst of the chaos, the Rightwing minions claimed:

- The Obama administration watched the attacks unfold in real time from a drone circling above but did nothing to intervene;
- Requests issued by U.S. personnel at the embassy for military back-up during the attacks were denied;
- General Carter Ham was relieved of his command for attempting to provide military assistance during the Benghazi attacks;
- Rear Admiral Charles M. Gaouette was relieved of his command for attempting to provide military assistance during the Benghazi attacks;

The first bullet-point is a distorted version of a CBS News story that ran the day of the attack. The report did not claim the Obama administration watched real-time video of developments from a drone circling over the embassy. Instead, it claimed a single diplomatic security official was listening to an audio feed of events in Benghazi. Security cameras in the consulate compound recorded video of the events as they unfolded, and a surveillance drone camera did capture the last hour of the attack, but neither of those sources were watched in real-time by officials in Washington.

The second bullet-point is based on a Fox News report released on October 26, 2012 claiming, urgent requests for military back-up from those on the ground during the attacks on the U.S. mission in Benghazi were turned down by the CIA chain-of-command. On the contrary, the U.S. Senate Select Committee on Intelligence on January 15, 2014, reviewed viewed video footage documenting the dispatch of a security team to the compound within 20-25 minutes of the first report of the attack, and they found that no "stand down" orders were issued to the security team at the Annex. Thus, revealing Fox News' irresponsible reporting habits.

The third bullet-point is based on distortions surrounding the upcoming retirement of General Carter Ham, the head of the U.S. Africa Command during the Benghazi attacks. On October 18, 2012, President Obama announced he had selected a nominee to replace General Ham as commander of the U.S. Africa command. General Ham testified before the House Committee on Armed Services in June 2013 stating, he never attempted to send troops to Benghazi. The decision not to deploy close air support during the attack was made by him based on his assessment of the situation at the time, not because he was ordered to "stand down".

The forth bullet point is based on distortions surrounding the dismissal of Rear Admiral Charles M. Gaouette, commander of an air craft carrier strike group deployed in the Middle-East. But him being relieved of his command had nothing to do with the September 2012 attacks on U.S. facilities in Benghazi. On the contrary, it was because a complaint about his "unprofessional demeanor" had been filed against him by the USS John C. Stennis' commanding officer, Capt. Ronald Reis. A subsequent Navy investigation reprimanded Gaouette for repeatedly violating U.S. Navy policy by making and sending offensive comments via e-mail.

Did Republicans Orchestrate Benghazi?

Senator Barbara Boxer (D-CA) posted on her blog (May 13, 2013): *If my Republican colleagues are serious about conducting real oversight on the tragedy in Benghazi, they should start by looking in* *the mirror. Their first order of business should be examining the abhorrent cuts that House Republicans made to our State Department's embassy security budget -- cuts that put American lives at risk. The truth is -- between fiscal years 2011 and 2012, the Republican-led House of Representatives sought to cut more than $450-million from President Obama's budget request for embassy security funding. Although the Senate was able to restore some of this critical funding, it was not enough.*

Rather than taking responsibility for the budget cuts that they championed -- cuts that former Secretary of State Hillary Clinton warned would be "detrimental to America's national security" -- Republicans are desperately trying to create a political scandal in an effort to hurt the Administration and Hillary Clinton in particular, for obvious reasons ... Republicans tried and failed during the 2012 presidential election to use this tragedy for political gain and now appear eager to recycle these failed attacks.

In addition, Senator Boxer said in a speech before the Senate:
It takes funding to protect an embassy. It takes funding to protect a consulate. It takes funding to protect an outpost. Yes, it takes funding. Who cut the funds from embassy security? The Republicans in the House, that is who — hundreds of millions of dollars. If it were not for the Democrats, it would have been cut more, because when it came here, we stood our ground. We had to accommodate their cuts. That is how the process works. So I think the Benghazi 'scandal' starts with the Republicans looking in the mirror. Mirror, mirror, who is the fairest of them all? They ought to ask: Mirror, mirror, who cut the funding for diplomatic security across this world for America? The answer: Republicans.

What are the chances Republicans, in their campaign to make President Obama a one-term president, orchestrated Benghazi to fall on September 11, 2012, in a *failed attempt* to create a 911 for President Obama just short of 2-months prior to the November 2012 presidential election?

1) Mitt Romney never had a chance of winning! ... Ever!
2) At the time, Mitt Romney polled "extremely low" in every poll!

3) Is this something Republicans are incapable of? After all, these are people who do not hesitate to "rig presidential elections"! Benghazi was part of rigging the 2012 presidential election by creating a fake 911 scandal for President Obama.
4) Since the Republican ploy did not work, they scurried to blame everyone else (including UN Ambassador Susan Rice, Secretary of State Hillary Clinton and finally, President Obama) and eradicate any evidence that led to the Republican doorstep! This included getting a Reichwing committee to investigate and produce a report that claimed "Republican budget cuts had nothing to do with downsizing the security personnel".

Republicans claim their "budget cuts" had nothing to do with downsizing Benghazi personnel. But isn't it amazing every time you hear the words "budget cuts" in Corporate America the next thing everyone expects is "downsizing"? But this magically does not happen when with Republican budget cuts. Perhaps, Republican politicians should be running private corporations!

Great Depression, On Purpose?

To say the least, I think I have established a "behavior pattern" that identifies the demographic I commonly refer to as Rightwing advocates or the Rightwing minions. They typically display actions and deeds that don't fall short of a sociopath (one who is affected with a personality disorder marked by anti-social behavior). Is the average Rightwing advocate a sociopath? Do they believe beyond all rationale and reason that a handful of rich people should control all this country's wealth and resources? Hence, they believe the masses should have nothing (or close to nothing) and struggle for survival on a daily basis? Smells like anti-social behavior to me! Now, if Rightwing advocates are sociopaths, they should have a track record that indicates the same. Let's examine their history!

The "largest piece" of historical evidence identifying Rightwing sociopathic, anti-social behavior patterns is commonly referred to as *"The Great Depression"*. Often portrayed as an unavoidable accident, the details preceding it say different. The decade that preceded the Great Depression is nicknamed, *"The Roaring*

Twenties". It was called this to identify the 1920s decade as one of great prosperity. But what exactly caused such a surge in the U.S. economy that so many people prospered practically overnight? Well, when the economy is bad, we typically blame the people (and political party) running the government. Who was in-charge?

Now, please note when I say "Republicans" or the "Republican Party", there are two different types, identifying two different eras. The first is the *(Abraham Lincoln) Republican Party*, that started its beginnings in 1854, had <u>northern liberal ideals</u> and waved the American flag. The second is the *(Confederate) Republican Party*, that the (Lincoln) Republican Party evolved into at some point after 1866, that holds <u>Southern Confederate Democrat values</u> as they wave the Confederate flag. From this point forward, unless I say otherwise, when I use the term "Republican" or "Republican Party", I am referring to the latter (Confederate) Republicans, who's actions depict Southern Confederate Democrat values.

The 1920 presidential election was the beginning of a Republican agenda that resulted in the 1929 stock market crash and the great depression that followed. Through strategy massive campaign spending, the Republican candidates, *Warren G. Harding* and *Calvin Coolidge*, won a landslide victory against Democratic candidates, *James M. Cox* and *Franklin D. Roosevelt*. The electoral college vote was 404 to 127, respectively; 266 electoral college votes was needed to win. The main theme of the Republican agenda was what we now call *"deregulation"*. This is when Republicans remove "government regulations" from banks, business practices and wall street. But what Republicans always fail to mention is the fact, those government regulations they're so keen on getting rid of contains all the *consumer protection laws*. Hence, banks, businesses and stock brokers are allowed to do whatever they can dream up to make a profit, which typically means taking complete advantage (and at the expense) of unsuspecting consumers.

In August of 1923, President Harding suddenly died from what was believed at the time to be pneumonia; Vice-President Coolidge then became the president to continue the Republican agenda in action. Calvin Coolidge was President of the United States from August 1923 to March 1929, throughout most of the roaring twenties.

During which it was typical for the average Joe to easily borrow large sums from banks at very low interest rates, then place their bets in the stock market with the borrowed money. During the 1920s decade, millions of average Joes profited handsomely practically overnight, primarily from flooding the stock market with (low interest rate) borrowed money. This is also where the expression, *"spending other people's money (to profit)"*, originated; in capitalism. Businesses and banks boomed one-thousand fold from having no government regulations to interfere with (or put a cap on) their profits! Whatever they dreamt up, whatever the risk, was perfectly legal. Life was bliss for the those who benefited.

About eight months after Republican candidate *Herbert Hoover* took office (in March) after winning the 1928 presidential election ... *Hey, the economy was booming and Republicans were the reason! Herbert Hoover beat the Democratic challenger Al Smith in a 444 to 87 electoral college vote landslide victory; 266 electoral college votes were needed to win* ... it all came to a screeching halt when the stock market crashed (in November) and everyone lost everything! Everyone except for about 20% of the population.

Another item of the Republican agenda is to create a society where a small segment of wealthy people own and control everything. This is an Southern Democrat idea that goes even further back than the Confederate States of America; an 16th century idea that existed in England that created the system of slavery for the dirt poor masses that came to the American colonies! So, by 1930 about 10% of the population profited from the stock market crash, another 10% could be considered the new middle-class, and the vast majority, the remaining 80%, either lived in poverty or close to it. This was the ideal society Republicans wanted to achieve. So, was the era of prosperity that preceded it merely a smoke screen? While everyone was busy being star stricken by good fortune, they never saw the inevitable collapse coming.

Now, the stock market did not crash because of anything President Hoover began during his presidency, as much as, because of the nine years of Republican policies that preceded him. Be that as it may, in an effort to combat the downward spiral in the economy, President Hoover increased the tax bracket of the rich (the only people who had anything) from 25% to 63%. But this noble effort did not bear any fruit before the 1932 presidential election, in which Democratic challenger Franklin D. Roosevelt defeated the incumbent Herbert Hoover in a landslide 472 to 59 electoral college vote victory; 266 electoral college votes was needed to win. And he also won a Democratic Congress! Along with the presidency, Republicans controlled Congress from the 66th Congress (beginning March 1919) to the 71st Congress (ending March 1931).

So, Republican President Herbert Hoover's administration (March 1929 to March 1933) paralleled the 72nd Congress (March 1931 to March 1933); during which Republicans controlled the Senate but Democrats now controlled the House of Representatives. This was the beginning sign of the Republicans, having been blamed for the stock market crash and the depressing economy, being voted out! In comparison, Democrat Franklin D. Roosevelt's first term (March 1933 to March 1937) paralleled the 73rd Congress (March 1933 to January 1935) and 74th Congress (January 1935 to January 1937), during which Democrats controlled both the Senate and the House of Representatives. In his first 100 days in office, Roosevelt spearheaded major legislation and issued a plethora of executive orders that established the *New Deal* (a variety of federal programs designed to produce *relief* (government jobs for the unemployed), *recovery* (economic growth), and *reform* (through regulation of banks, businesses and the stock market); a.k.a. *The Three R's*.

Republican deregulation of banks, businesses and the stock market throughout the 1920s led to the stock market crash of 1929 and the great depression (crash of banks and businesses) of the 1930s. The Democratic implement of federal regulations for banks, businesses and the stock market to prevent them from running amuck and running the economy into the ground is what saved the economy. The American people were so grateful to Franklin D. Roosevelt for dragging them out of an economic depression, he was elected three times! Roosevelt's first term was from 1933 to 1937; his second term, 1937 to 1941; and his third term, 1941 to 1945. The 22nd Amendment, setting the term limits to two did not exist until 1947. Since Roosevelt enjoyed a Democratic controlled Congress, there was nothing to stop his first New Deal legislation in 1933 nor his second New Deal legislation in 1934, during which

Roosevelt signed the Glass–Steagall Act that created the *Federal Deposit Insurance Corporation* (FDIC).

The Glass–Steagall Act was banking legislation named after its Congressional sponsors, Senator *Carter Glass* [D] of Virginia, and Representative *Henry B. Steagall* [D] of Alabama. The basis of the legislation was to:

1) limit the securities activities for commercial banks
2) limit affiliations between commercial banks and securities firms
3) when people made bank deposits, insure their money

Both New Deals basically put "government" everywhere and in everything. This helped most of the 80% of Americans who were living in poverty or close to it during the depression years to stand on their own two feet by providing jobs and federal assistance programs; for individuals, businesses and farmers. And in those days, nobody frowned on help from the federal government.

Fast forward eight presidential elections to 1980, where Republican challenger *Ronald Reagan* defeated Democratic incumbent *Jimmy Carter* in a 489 to 49 electoral college victory; 270 electoral college votes were needed to win. In addition, Republicans won control of Congress! What did this resemble? The Roaring Twenties all over again! Was it? You decide! Republicans (during the Reagan era, 1981-1989) began to gradually dismantle all the federal regulations put in place by Franklin D. Roosevelt and temporary middle-class prosperity was everywhere, again! But when President Reagan deregulated banking in 1982, the banking industry collapse! But instead of putting the federal regulations back in place that would permanently repair the damage, Republican's kept the banks deregulated with a temporarily $1.3-billion Taxpayer Bailout band-aid. This held everything together until 2007.

This Republican agenda continued during the George H.W. Bush era (1989-1993). It also continued during the Bill Clinton era, the six years he had a Republican Congress (1995-2001). Finally, this Republican agenda sealed the deal during the George W. Bush era (2001-2008). The first signs of collapse began to show in 2006 and Republicans were voted out of congressional control in that year's midterm elections. To circumvent his new Democratic Congress,

Bush issued about 70 Executive Orders between January 2007 and January 2009. Hence, the notion his hands were tied during his last two years in office is a bunch of hogwash! Be that as it may, after Democrat *Barack H. Obama's* 2009 inauguration, his first line of business was to reinstall the federal regulations created during the Franklin D. Roosevelt administration that fixed the first great depression. Republicans have been trying to sneak "Republican deregulation" back on American society under new names.

The National Debt, Explained

The national debt is the *total amount of money owed* by the federal government to creditors who hold U.S. debt instruments (treasury bills, savings bonds). This includes all federal debt held by states, corporations, individuals and foreign governments and is the accumulation of money owed by every previous administration. The federal deficit is created when the current administration spends more money than it earns (beyond the federal budget) within a fiscal year (October 1st current year to September 30th the following year). When an administration ends with a federal deficit, it is added to the total national debt.

The President creates a *budget proposal* based on what his administration estimates government spending will cost over the next fiscal year. This process begins on the first Monday in February and ends on October 1st. The president sends his vision to Congress, who then begins to chip away at it, creating its own version (budget resolution). The House of Representatives and the Senate must come up with matching resolutions, resulting in a Spending Bill. The President then signs the bill signaling the end of the process. If they fail to meet the deadline, the government has no money to function and it automatically shuts down.

Now, there are two different kinds of federal debt; public and intra-governmental (private). Public debt (65% of national debt) is all the money owed to the public via U.S. treasury bonds, bills and savings bonds). Intra-governmental debt consists of all the money the government owes itself from borrowing against pools of governmental pools of money (i.e. social security trust fund). The total outstanding national debt as of this writing is $17.5-trillion.

The national debt became a hot topic after the George W. Bush administration ended. The non-partisan economist *Mike Kimel* notes, through in-depth research, the former Democratic Presidents (*Bill Clinton, Jimmy Carter, Lyndon B. Johnson, John F. Kennedy,* and *Harry S. Truman*) all reduced national debt as a share of Gross Domestic Product while the last four Republican Presidents (*George W. Bush, George H.W. Bush, Ronald Reagan,* and *Gerald Ford*) all oversaw an increase in the country's indebtedness. When the George W. Bush administration began (January 20, 2001), the national debt was $5.73-trillion; and when it ended (January 20, 2009), the debt was $10.63-trillion. Hence, during the 8-year Bush administration, the national debt increased by $4.87-trillion.

Although Barack Obama was inaugurated on January 20, 2009, the $3.1-trillion FY2009 budget was submitted, negotiated, and signed into law by former-President George W. Bush by October 1, 2008. President Obama's first budget was the FY2010; an October 1, 2009 deadline; the national debt was $11.92-trillion. Hence, the $1.29-trillion difference between 20 January 2009 and 1 October 2009 is from the FY2009 budget that George W. Bush in 2008. FYI: The $3.1-trillion FY2009 budget was divided: $1.21-trillion (public), $1.89-trillion (private: Medicare, Medicaid, Social Security, Unemployment). Contrary to Republican math, the Obama administration is only responsible for $3.98-trillion of the $17.5-trillion national debt beginning with the FY2010 budget. And as the records state, the George W. Bush administration is responsible for adding $6.16-trillion to the national debt.

Contrary to popular belief, "the amount" of the national debt is not the problem. For example, your personal total debt situation is based on your total income. Our nation's total debt is no different! Typically, a person with an annual income of $150,000 will have more debt than a person with an annual income of $40,000. But does that put the person with the higher income in a worse debt situation? A country's annual income is called the *Gross Domestic Product* (GDP) and it complements the country's total debt. As long as there is a healthy balance between the national debt and the national income, the economy will be in good standing.

In economics, the *"debt-to-GDP ratio"* (debt divided-by GDP) shows the state of the economy; the lower the ratio the better. In September 2013, when the Tea Party was busy trying to defund Obamacare by shutting down the federal government, the national debt was $16.7-trillion, the GDP was 16.8-trillion, and the debt-to-GDP ratio was 99%. Since then (with the new spending bill), our current debt-to-GDP ratio increased to 101%. Once again, this is the ratio of the national debt in December 2013 ($17.3-trillion) divided by the GDP in December 2013 ($17.1-trillion). As you can now see, it is not the amount of the national debt we should be concerned about as much as it is the debt-to-GDP ratio.

Although, our current debt-to-GDP ratio of 101% is high, this is not the highest its ever been. The highest debt-to-GDP ratio was recorded in 1947 @ 121.7%. But it obviously did not stay there; it came down over time. The lowest was recorded in 1975 @ 31.7%. The Rightwing minions are taught to whine about the amount of the national debt "$17-TRILLION" as though our economy is on the verge of collapse all over again! But if history does repeat itself, the debt-to-GDP ratio will get lower over time, with a Democratic president in the White House.

The Debt Ceiling

The debt ceiling is basically "the limit" on how much "gross debt" the federal government can have, put another way, the statutory maximum of money the U.S. Treasury is allowed to borrow (via the sales of U.S. securities) on the behalf of the federal government. Once the debt ceiling is set, the Treasury is free to borrow whatever the federal government needs as long as it does not go past the ceiling (or limit) set by Congress. During the 2011 Debt Ceiling Crisis, President Obama said, *"Raising the debt ceiling does not allow Congress to spend more money. It simply gives our country the ability to pay the bills that Congress has already racked up."* Congress has raised the debt ceiling 78-times since 1960; and all without incident. Why was it such a big deal in 2011?

First of all, the Republican Party had been stewing over the fact Democrat Barack Obama won the 2008 presidential election. Fast forward two years, Republicans won the House of Representatives and ever since, they did nothing but try to prevent President Obama from accomplishing anything. One year later it was time for the Spending Bill negotiations during which House Republicans demanded that the President negotiate over deficit reduction in exchange for an increase in the debt ceiling. Note, no other prior president ever had to negotiate over raising the debt ceiling.

Before we move on, here's a brief history of debt ceiling increases:

RONALD REAGAN [R] (January'81-January'89):
1) February 1981 - $**985** billion
2) September 1981 - $**999.8** billion
3) September 1981 - $**1.0798** trillion
4) June 1982 - $**1.1431** trillion
5) September 1982 - $**1.2902** trillion
6) May 1983 - $**1.389** trillion
7) November 1983 - $**1.49** trillion
8) May 1984 - $**1.52** trillion
9) July 1984 - $**1.573** trillion
10) October 1984 - $**1.8238** trillion
11) November 1985 - $**1.9038** trillion
12) December 1985 - $**2.0787** trillion
13) August 1986 - $**2.111** trillion
14) October 1986 - $**2.3** trillion
15) May 1987 - $**2.32** trillion
16) July 1987 - $**2.32** trillion
17) August 1987 - $**2.352** trillion
18) September 1987 - $**2.8** trillion

GEORGE H. W. BUSH [R] (January'89-January'93):
1) August 1989 - $**2.87** trillion
2) November 1989 - $**3.1227** trillion
3) August 1990 - $**3.195** trillion
4) October 1990 - $**3.23** trillion
5) November 1990 - $**4.145** trillion

BILL CLINTON [D] (January'93-January'01):
1) April 1993 - $**4.37** trillion
2) August 1993 - $**4.9** trillion

3) March 1996 - **$5.5** trillion
4) August 1997 - **$5.95** trillion

GEORGE W. BUSH [R] (January'01-January'09):
1) June 2002 - **$6.4** trillion
2) May 2003 - **$7.384** trillion
3) November 2004 - **$8.184** trillion
4) March 2006 - **$8.965** trillion
5) September 2007 - **$9.815** trillion
6) July 2008 - **$10.615** trillion
7) October 2008 - **$11.315** trillion

BARACK OBAMA [D] (January'09-Present):
February 2009 - **$12.104** trillion
December 2009 - **$12.394** trillion
February 2010 - **$14.294** trillion
August 2011 - **$14.694** trillion
September 2011 - **$16.394** trillion

According to the US Treasury's Monthly Statement of Public Debt:

Ronald Reagan's administration began with $848-**b**illion total debt and ended with $2.698-**t**rillion; an increase of **218.1**%.

George H.W. Bush's administration began with $2.698-trillion total debt and ended with $4.188-trillion; an increase of **55.22**%.

Bill Clinton's administration began with $4.188-trillion and ended with $5.728-trillion; an increase of 36.77%.

George W. Bush's administration began with $5.728-trillion in total debt and ended with $10.627-trillion; an increase of **85.52**%.

Barack Obama's administration began with $10.627-trillion in total debt and ended with $16.432-trillion; an increase of 54.62%.

Even with a collapsing economy, the increase at the end of President Obama's first term was lower than George H.W. Bush's one term in office when the economy was flourishing; 54.62% to 55.22%. And Bill Clinton's two terms ended with a much lower increase than Ronald; 36.77% to 218.1%. Believe it or not, Republican politicians and strategists know these details. Hence, these are the main motivations behind Rightwing rhetoric; which says the complete opposite about the Democrat. For instance, Barack Obama's great fiscal record is the reason the Rightwing minions are programmed to call him the worst president ever!

The Fiscal Cliff

Many of us hear the term "fiscal cliff" for the very first time about two years after Barack Obama's 2009 inauguration. Why, you might ask? Simply put, Republicans were on the warpath; still fuming over having lost the 2008 presidential election! The powers-that-be behind the Republican Party (Heritage Foundation) created obstacles at every point of the Obama administration's roadmap their sinister imaginations could dream up! Before we tackle the fiscal cliff, let's review a few more terms:

Fiscal Year (FY): The financial year (or budget year) the federal government uses to calculate its annual budget for the next year; beginning October 1st of the current year and ending September 30th of the following year.

National Debt: The total amount of *gross public debt* owed by the United States government; a measure of the Treasury securities that are currently outstanding. Gross public debt is divided into *Public* (65%, Treasury securities (bills, notes, and bonds) held by investors outside the federal government: individuals, corporations, states and foreign countries) and *Intergovernmental/non-public* (35%, non-marketable Treasury securities (savings bonds) held in accounts administered by the federal government (Social Security Trust Fund)); money the federal government owes itself.

Nobody really cares about money the federal government owes itself. Hence, most of the time Republicans use the term "national debt", they are only referring to the "public debt" portion (money owed to investors outside the federal government); but for sinister reasons they announce the combined amounts! For instance, currently the total national debt is $17.3-trillion, but only $11.2-trillion of it is public debt owed to investors outside the federal government; the other $6.05-trillion is money the government owes its own internal operations.

Gross Domestic Product (GDP): The market value of all the goods and services a country produces in a given period of time (a nation's income); typically one year.

Debt-to-GDP Ratio: the ratio (the amount of times one number contains the other number) between government (national) debt and its gross domestic product (how many times the amount of the GDP can go into the amount of the national debt); typically expressed in a percentage. The lower the percentage, the more an economy can pay back its debts without incurring further debt. Now, when determining the debt-to-GDP ratio, should we use the amount of the gross public debt ($17.3-trillion) or the amount of the public debt ($11.2-trillion)?

Typically, no one really cares about the non-public debt. Hence, should we only use the public debt in the debt-to-GDP ratio calculation? In a previous chapter we used the gross public debt, $17.3-trillion divided by the 2013 GDP, $17.1-trillion to get a ratio of 101%. But suppose we remained true to the portion of the national debt (public debt) that we're really concerned about paying off? This changes the equation to $11.2-trillion divided by the GDP, $17.1-trillion, resulting in a ratio of $65.5%. You decide!

Federal Budget: The President's proposal to Congress suggesting the funding levels for the next fiscal year. Congress is the body required by law to pass an annual budget, negotiate the details with the Senate, then submit the approved budget to the President to sign. If this final version drastically strays from the President's original proposal, the president may "veto" until a more respectable compromise can be reached. You may also hear this topic referred to as *"government spending"*.

Federal Budget Deficit (National Deficit, Federal Deficit, Budget Deficit): Often referred to as *"the deficit"* is often confused with the "National Debt". In layman's terms, a deficit happens when the government's spending exceeds its income. In FY2014 (1 Oct 2013 – 30 Sept 2014), the federal budget deficit is projected to be $284-billion. This is only because the FY2014 federal budget is $3.318-trillion and the projected government revenue (income) is $3.034-trillion. But for the record, this is the lowest deficit since the 2008 recession, and is tiny compared to the record FY2009 (1 Oct 2008 – 30 Sept 2009) budget deficit of $1.4-trillion.

The national debt is an accumulation of the federal budget deficits dating back to 1790. Thomas Jefferson (the first Secretary of State) wanted to pay off the national debt incurred from the Revolutionary War after the U.S. Constitution was in place and the newly formed government could now collect taxes. But Alexander Hamilton (the first Secretary of Treasury), an experienced banker, pointed out that by keeping the debt, the country's credibility would increase as the nation prospered and production increased. Hence, Hamilton stabilized the dollar and refunded all the state debts incurred in the Revolutionary War by refinancing them as an obligation of the new federal government. The resulting federal debt stood at 35% of GDP.

Debt Ceiling ((Statutory) Debt Limit): The maximum amount of money the federal government can borrow. Created under the Second Liberty Bond Act of 1917, this bill put a "ceiling" on the amount of bonds the Treasury can issue on behalf of the federal government. The Treasury Department keeps track of government spending and decides a deadline for when the debt ceiling should be raised or the statutory borrowing limit, increased. Both houses of Congress (the House of Representatives and the Senate) then race to negotiate as to how far to raise the debt ceiling before the deadline. Or put another way, before the federal government runs out of money to meet its financial obligations.

Now understand, the U.S. dollar is the most widely accepted form of currency in the world. And investment in U.S. securities (t-bills, t-bonds, t-notes) is considered to be one of the safest investments in the world because of the international acceptance of US dollar. This is based on two strong assumptions: 1) the U.S. government will not default on its loans and will always pay back the sum assured; 2) the U.S. dollar will continue to be a popular and universally accepted currency. If either of these assumptions become unreliable, the global financial market will lose faith in U.S. treasury issued security bonds. Raising the debt ceiling makes sure this does not happen. And Republicans who use the debt ceiling as a means of extortion are extremely unpatriotic!

Fiscal Cliff: This is the popular shorthand term used to describe the conundrum the federal government faced at the end of 2012, when the terms of the *Budget Control Act of 2011* were scheduled to go into effect. Remember that? Of course you don't! But you do probably remember the debt ceiling crisis that happened in 2011. Approximately, one year after the Republican Party took control of the House of Representatives after the 2010 midterms, House Republicans demanded that President Obama negotiate over *"deficit reduction"* in exchange for an increase in the debt ceiling. Understand, Republicans were still stewing over the fact their candidate lost the 2008 presidential election. No other president before Barack Obama ever had to negotiate an increase in the debt ceiling; Congress just did it because it was necessary.

If government spending broach the debt ceiling, the Treasury would have to default on its financial obligations. And since a large part of those obligations include paying millions of securities that matured, owned by foreign individual investors, companies and countries, it would have led to a significant international financial crisis. As it turned out, two days prior to July 31st deadline set by the Treasury department (the federal government would run out of money to function), Republicans agreed to raise the debt ceiling in exchange for a complex deal of significant future spending cuts. Later that week, the credit-rating agency Standard & Poor's downgraded the credit rating of the United States government for the first time in its history. The *Government Accountability Office* (GAO) estimated that the delay in raising the debt ceiling increased government borrowing costs by $1.3-billion in 2011. Republicans never think about the damage they do when they do what they do.

By August 3, 2011, the federal government would officially default on its financial obligations. President Obama signed the Budget Control Act of 2011 into law on August 2, 2011, bringing an end to the debt ceiling crisis. This agreement required Congress to form a bipartisan Super Committee to slash $1.2-trillion in spending cuts over 10-years by November 23, 2011. Otherwise, there would be automatic across-the-board spending cuts proportionate to the size of each government agency and program, to take place beginning January 1, 2013. On November 21st, the committee concluded its work, issuing the following statement: *"After months of hard work and intense deliberations, we have come to the conclusion today that it will not be possible to make any bipartisan agreement available to the public before the committee's deadline."* The committee was formally terminated on January 31, 2012 and the spending cuts were scheduled to begin at midnight on December 31, 2012 or January 1, 2013.

Just three hours before the midnight deadline, the Senate agreed to a deal to avert the fiscal cliff. Although, the Senate version of the bill passed two hours after midnight, the House version passed 21-hours later. Hence, the federal government technically went "over the cliff," since the final details were not hashed out until after the beginning of the New Year.

The Sequester: A partial resolution to the fiscal cliff, addressing the automatic spending cuts that were initially set to begin on January 1, 2013, but were postponed for two months by the *American Taxpayer Relief Act of 2012*. A bill actually, approved by Congress on January 1, 2013 and signed into law by President Obama on January 2, 2013. These harmful spending cuts began on March 1, 2013. The $85.3-billion sequestration includes:

$42.7 billion in defense cuts (7.7% cut)
$26.1 billion in domestic discretionary cuts (5.1% cut)
$11.1 billion in Medicare cuts (2% cut)
$5.4 billion in other mandatory cuts (5.2% cut)

The Worst President Ever?

The Rightwing minions are batting 100 when it comes to spouting unfounded statements. I made it a habit to perform my own investigations and do my own research whenever I hear the Rightwing minions regurgitate an accusation. As it turns out, President Obama managed to accomplish quite a bit without the help of the Republican Party of Vote No. According to a *Rachel Maddow* report (of the Rachel Maddow Show on MSNBC), President Obama accomplished 85% of his first term agenda by the end of 2010. During the first 2-years of the Obama administration, he:

- Reduce the world's nuclear stockpiles
- Lock down loose nuclear materials (to not fall into the wrong hands)
- Healthcare Reform; The Affordable Care Act
- Children's Health Insurance
- Rebuilding Our Economy Recovery Act
- Wall Street Reform

- Middle-Class Tax Cuts
- Credit Card Reform
- Repealed Don't Ask Don't Tell
- Building A Clean-Energy Economy
- Rebuilding The American Auto Industry
- National Security Ending Combat Operations In Iraq
- Toward A World Without Nuclear Weapons
- A New Strategy For Afghanistan And Pakistan
- Education Reforming Student Lending
- Spurring Innovation
- A New GI Bill

After the 2010 midterm elections, President Obama lost his 60 vote majority in the Senate and the Democratic control of the House of Representatives and he still managed to pass major legislation. In the words of Rachel Maddow, *"The past two years have been historic, yet a small vocal minority of Obama's base is upset with this president and the nation as a whole tends to give him little credit for what he has done. It would be easy to blame his supporters and the American people for not paying attention, but that isn't an accurate portrayal of what's going on here. The problem is that Obama is not interested in victory laps, and publicly taking credit for his accomplishments. Obama wants to get things done, but the President has hopefully learned the hard lesson that if he doesn't sell his own accomplishments, his opponents are more than happy to use the media to distort and tear them down."*

This is exactly what Rightwing excel in doing! Fox News has been on a mission from day one of the Obama administration to convince its viewers, President Obama has not done a thing since he's been in office. Even when they do acknowledge something the president has done, it's in a negative manner. And of course, if the extreme Right never agrees with what the President is doing, they don't recognize it as an achievement. Especially, when all the Republican Party has done since Barack Obama's inauguration is "vote no" to try to prevent him from doing anything. And then when something doesn't get done, the Right acts like THEY had nothing to do with that thing not getting done.

Perhaps, one of the best things that happened for President Obama was the Republican Party taking the House of Representatives after the 2010 midterm elections. From January 2009 to October 2010, Republicans were effectively blaming everything under the sun on President Obama. It didn't matter whether or not the accusations were true; the Republicans were perceived as the underdogs! But winning the House, Republicans only managed to put themselves back into the spotlight. Hence, they could no longer effectively blame every little thing on President Obama and appear innocent. And about two months after the Republican Party takeover, the approval rating of Congress dropped to 13%. A very good sign the American people were not blaming the President for every little thing. This was also a very good sign the blame was being directed to the proper source; the Republican Party of No!

After the entire country witnessed the GOP and Tea Party fighting like cats and dogs at the 2011 Debt Ceiling negotiations and nearly pushing the country to the brink of default, the Republican Party's approval rating dropped from 41% to 33%; and the Tea Party joined that decline going from 37% to 31%. After this debacle, the Democratic Party was a little more appreciated and got a 2% boost in their approval rating, going from 45% to 47%. Unfortunately, according to some polls, President Obama's approval rating dropped to 41%. Fox News had a hay day claiming, *"Obama's approval rating hit an all time low!"* But putting things in perspective, President Obama's "all time low" was still 8-points higher than the Republican Party's all time low of 33% and 10-points higher than the Tea Party's 31%. Then again, when we're talking about the President of the United States, one poll doesn't quite cut it! A single poll is more like a "personal opinion" when there are 99 other polls with different results. The poll average of all the polls is a more accurate assessment; and President Obama's polling average is always around 50%.

It has always been an opinion of mine, the Republican Party (and their Rightwing minions) cannot see any further than the nose on their face. Is it at all remotely possible the 2010 midterms turned out exactly the way President Obama wanted it to turn out? Could he be a political genius who saw the benefit of a Republican House? After all, the Republican Party has only plummeted after they took control of the House of Representatives. To date, their approval rating is 28%. They obviously did not realize, after the George W. Bush administration, everything Republicans do (or did not do) would now be under a magnifying glass of scrutiny. This is one of the main reasons, Republicans are quick to point the finger of accusation in another direction when they are the real culprits!

Republicans call President Obama the worse president ever, so you don't look at Republican presidents! In contrast to President Obama, Ronald Reagan is the architect of Republican deregulation. He removed many of the fundamental and pragmatic banking regulations put in place after the devastating financial collapses of the earlier Great Depression of the 1930s. For decades, federal regulations served to strengthen banks, making them the envy of the world. But after many major banking regulations were removed, Savings & Loans scandals began to pop up because unethical people took complete advantage of the lack of rules.

Some economists even suggest Reagan's deregulation policies are what gave birth to the 2008 financial crisis. Republicans pretend collapsing something as enormous and complicated as the U.S. economy is capable of collapsing after only one or two years of Democratic policies. The truth of the matter, the U.S. economy will eventually collapse after decades of Republican deregulation beginning with the Reagan administration. Was Ronald Reagan the worse president ever? If he isn't, he could be a contender! If the Reagan administration is reduced to a snapshot you find:

- 31 convictions, including:
 • 14 because of Iran-Contra
 • 16 in the Department of Housing & Urban Development scandal
- 40 government officials indicted/convicted in the wake of the Watergate scandal
 • 14 individuals/businesses convicted/pleaded guilty to crimes
-61 indictments or misdemeanor charges
 • 14 persons were imprisoned
 • 138 administration officials had been convicted, indicted, or were investigated for official misconduct and/or criminal violations

- 4 members of the Reagan cabinet came under criminal investigation

- the Savings & Loan debacle which cost taxpayers $1.3-billion

And let's not even begin to talk about how Republican President Richard M. Nixon's administration (1969-1974) ended with the Watergate scandal! Eventually, the George W. Bush administration (2001-2008) gave us:

- the terrorist attack on the WTC on September 11, 2001;
- the war in Iraq
- the war in Afghanistan
- the collapse of the banking industry
- the collapse of the auto industry
- the collapse of the housing industry
- the collapse of the stock market
- the outsourcing of millions US jobs to overseas locations
- the downsizing of millions of US workers
- rising unemployment
- rising national debt
- billions in taxpayer bailouts to the private sector

Although, some of the items listed were seeded long before the Bush administration, it still gets blamed because so many other things happened simultaneously. The aforementioned Republican presidents are the main motivations behind Fox News' constant attempts to stick fake scandals to President Obama.

Finally, the title of "worst president ever" most definitely should not be determined by personal and biased opinion but rather according to the final overall approval ratings; which president had the worst compared to which president had the best.

George W. Bush Approval Rating = 22%
Richard M. Nixon Approval Rating = 24%
Jimmy Carter Approval Rating = 44%
George H. W. Bush Approval Rating = 54%
Barack Obama Approval Rating = 54% (currently)
Ronald Reagan Approval Rating = 68%
Bill Clinton Approval Rating = 68%

George W. Bush's final approval rating is the lowest final rating for an outgoing president since Gallup began asking about presidential approval more than 70 years ago. Does this make him the official worst president, ever? You decide!

Rule #1: Always Blame The Dems!

Logic would dictate, the thing that caused the U.S. economy to collapse in 2008 the second time was the same thing that caused the U.S. economy to collapse in 1929 the first time. To explore this logic, I examined the events that preceded the 1929 stock market crash and the 1930's great depression that followed. The only consistent culprit was the "Republican deregulation" of business, banks and wall street. Republicans controlled the White House and both houses of Congress from 1921 to 1933; and controlled both houses of Congress from 1919 to 1931. As these years reveal, the Republican Party was voted out of the White House and Congress shortly after the stock market crashed in 1929. Hence, I am not the only one who thinks Republicans were responsible!

Be that as it may, this did not stop the Republican powers-that-be to teach the Rightwing minions, differently! The Republican Party's #1 rule of engagement is to always blame what they did (and was responsible for) on the Democrats! At least all the negative stuff like collapsing the U.S. economy! I have heard a few of the claims they make, in attempts to blame the 2008 collapse on previous Democratic presidents. This chapter will review and examine the claims I have heard about. And if these can be debunked, so can the ones I haven't heard about!

Jimmy Carter Passed The CRA!

The CRA is an acronym for *The Community Reinvestment Act of 1977*. This fine piece of legislation was passed into law to address *discrimination* in loans made to individuals and businesses from low and moderate income neighborhoods. It mandated that all banking institutions that receive FDIC insurance be evaluated by Federal banking agencies to determine if the bank offers credit (in a manner consistent with safe and sound operation as per Section 802(b) and Section 804(1)) in all communities in which they are chartered to do business.

According to the extreme Rightwing, this (31-year old) legislation is responsible for approving mortgage loans, regardless of the size, to people who had no credit, no jobs, no down payment and no means to repay. Ergo, it created the house of cards that eventually collapsed the housing industry in 2008. However, Rightwing advocates fail to realize, the 1977 Community Reinvestment Act only applied to banks and savings & loans. Mortgage Lenders, not regulated by the CRA, took complete advantage of the deregulation of banks that began with Ronald Reagan. In 1982, Reagan signed the *Garn-St. Germain Depository Institutions Act*. This bill removed statutory restrictions on real estate lending, and relaxed limits on the amount that could be lent to a single borrower. Mortgage Lenders used "creative financing" schemes to do just about anything they could dream up!

The Savings & Loans Crisis!

It is highly likely we would have seen any detrimental effects of a law passed in 1977, little sooner than 31-years down the road in 2008. Reagan's deregulation program freed savings & loans from restrictions and his economic policies reduced the government regulations of private enterprise. In addition, savings & loans were allowed to make high-risk loans in astronomical amounts to individuals and businesses without risk to themselves. Hence, the taxpayers would insure these private loans in the same manner they insured mortgage loans. Hence, Republicans wanted the government (regulations) off the backs of business and at the same time wanted the government (and taxpayers) to insure business! Today, economists have learned *"lifting the restrictions on loans"* while *"leaving government insurance in place"* was (and still is) a recipe for disaster! After President Reagan deregulated the banking industry, multiple counts of fraud and corruption eventually developed and hundreds of savings & loans failed!

One of the most popular cases of fraud was given the moniker, *The Keating Five*. These five Senators were accused of corruption in 1989 for igniting a major political scandal as part of the larger savings & loan crisis: *Alan Cranston* (Democrat-CA), *Dennis DeConcini* (Democrat-AZ), *John Glenn* (Democrat-OH), *John McCain* (Republican-AZ), and *Donald W. Riegle, Jr.* (Democrat-MI). They were accused of improperly intervening in 1987 on behalf of

Charles H. Keating, Jr., Chairman of the Lincoln Savings & Loan Association, which was the target of a regulatory investigation by the Federal Home Loan Bank Board (FHLBB). Senators John Glenn and John McCain were cleared of having acted improperly.

In 1988, the Silverado Savings & Loan collapsed, costing a $1.3-billion taxpayer bailout. Neil Bush, son of George H.W. Bush, was on Silverado's Board of Directors. He was accused of giving himself a loan and voting to approve $100-million, in what were ultimately bad loans, to two of his business partners. In voting for the loans, Bush failed to inform fellow board members the loan applicants were his business partners. The U.S. Office of Thrift Supervision determined Neil Bush had engaged in numerous *"breaches of his fiduciary duties involving multiple conflicts of interest."* Although he was not indicted on criminal charges, a civil action was brought against him and the other Silverado directors by the FDIC. The case was eventually settled out of court, with Bush paying $50,000 as part of the settlement (paid for him by Republican supporters). Neil Bush was banned from banking activities and a suit by *Resolution Trust Corporation* was settled in 1991 for $26.5-million.

Bill Clinton Signed NAFTA!
NAFTA is an acronym for the *North America Fair Trade Act;* an agreement signed by the governments of Canada, Mexico, and the United States creating a trilateral trade bloc. You can tell NAFTA was a Republican bill once you realize what it did. In a nutshell, *NAFTA eliminated government-induced restrictions on international trade in North America.* Whoop, There it is! If a bill is lifting or removing "government regulations", it's a Republican bill. NAFTA removed trade barriers, customs duties and tariffs, over the course of 15-years, allowing manufactured goods and commodities to be freely traded among Canada, Mexico, and the United States.

Contrary to what Rightwing minions claim, the inspiration of NAFTA began with Ronald Reagan. Late in his first term (1981-1985), he campaigned for a North American common market. Congress passed the *Trade and Tariff Act* (1984) giving Reagan the authority to negotiate free trade agreements. Congress was only allowed to approve or disapprove the negotiating points; not change any of them. At the end of Reagan's 2nd term (1985-89), he went out swinging, still proposing free trade with Canada and Mexico.

In 1990-91 President George H.W. Bush picked up where Reagan left off, leading the NAFTA negotiations with Prime Minister *Brian Mulroney* (Canada) and President *Carlos Salinas* (Mexico). In 1991-92, the three leaders approved the first NAFTA draft. In October 1992, they attended the NAFTA Initialing Ceremony where the primary NAFTA negotiators of each country finalized the details. Unfortunately, Bush did not win his bid for re-election in November. Regardless, the three leaders signed the preliminary NAFTA draft pending ratification by the three legislatures in December 1992.

In January 1993, Bill Clinton was inaugurated the 42nd President of the United States. During his first year in office, he campaigned on behalf of NAFTA. In December, Clinton signed the final bill into law as a courtesy and good gesture to the Republicans who began the very lengthy process with Canada and Mexico approximately five years prior. Although he did not alter the original treaty, Clinton included the *North American Agreement on Labor Cooperation* and the *North American Agreement on Environmental Cooperation*. This made NAFTA the first "green" trade treaty and the first trade treaty concerned with each country's labor laws.

NAFTA is now considered the main source behind outsourcing U.S. jobs to overseas locations throughout the 1990's and early 2000's. As a result, Rightwing advocates completely ignore the 5-years Republican politicians exclusively worked on the bill and try to place the blame exclusively on Bill Clinton for signing the final draft. What Republicans have never done is acknowledge the fact that "Democrats (controlling the White House and both houses of Congress)" were in a position to annihilate NAFTA. But Democrats are not like Republicans who do things like "shut down when the government" when they are in a position to do so, out of spite. President Clinton had to consider the international relations with Canada and Mexico, as well as, the 5-years of work they also put into making NAFTA a reality.

Clinton Passed, Graham-Leach-Bliley Act
Rightwing advocates in the banking industry had been seeking the repeal of the *1933 Glass–Steagall Act* (federal regulations put in

place by Franklin D. Roosevelt during the Great Depression) since the Reagan administration. Republican Senator *Phil Gramm* first introduced a bill that would accomplish that very thing to the Senate in April 1999; the Republican controlled Senate passed the bill in May. Republican Congressmen *Jim Leach* and *Thomas J. Bliley, Jr.* then brought the bill to the Republican controlled House of Representatives; it passed with flying colors in July 1999. During the negotiations, Democrats argued, the bill would create banking conglomerates that would be "too big to fail" if they got into financial trouble and would require bailouts from the federal government to keep them in business. That's probably what Republicans were counting on!

In November 1999, the bill moved to a joint conference committee to work out the differences between the Senate and House versions. After this, it was signed into law by President Clinton. Hence, the Graham Leach Bliley Act was a Republican bill created by one Republican Senator and two Republican Congressmen; passed by a Republican controlled House and Senate; and finally, signed into law by a Democratic president. Why didn't Clinton put up a fight and join the Democrats in the House and Senate in challenging the bill? Because Republicans controlled the House of Representatives and the Senate to an extent they could get two-thirds "Yea" votes to support the bill. This would render the bill "veto proof"! Hence, whether the president signed the bill or not, it would become law! Clinton did the formability of signing the bill.

The Clinton Surplus

Rightwing advocates are notorious for not only blaming Democrats for everything Republicans did to hurt the U.S. economy, they also try to steal the credit for what Democrats did that helped the U.S. economy. For example, Rightwing advocates have been trying to steal the credit for the "Clinton surplus" since the beginning of the George W. Bush administration (2001)!

Bill Clinton presided over the longest period of peacetime economic expansion in American history. During his first two years, Clinton enjoyed a Democratic Congress; but Republicans won control in

1994 for the first time since the 83rd Congress (1953-1955). Two years later, Bill Clinton became the first Democratic to win a second term since Franklin D. Roosevelt (1933-1945). And at the end of his administration, the Congressional Budget Office (a nonpartisan entity) reported a federal budget surplus of $127.3-billion. As a reminder, this is the fiscal year budget of the federal government; not the national debt. The annual budget can either be balanced (spending = income), show a deficit (more spending than income), or show a surplus (more income than spending). In FY2000, the budget surplus was $236.4-billion; the largest in U.S. history! It topped the FY1999 record surplus of $125.6-billion and the FY1998 record of $69.2-billion.

For the record, Bill Clinton was not the first Democratic president to leave a budget surplus for an incoming Republican president. In 1969, Democratic president, Lyndon B. Johnson, exited the White House leaving a budget surplus of $3.2-billion for the incoming Republican president, Richard M. Nixon.

Clinton VS Gingrich
President Clinton's FY1995 budget (1 Oct 1994 to 30 Sept 1995), endorsed by the Democratic controlled 103rd Congress in October 1994, included a large tax increase that Republicans claimed was the largest in U.S. history; the tax burden fell mostly on the rich. However, the FY1996 budget was an entirely different matter. In the November 1994 midterm elections, Republicans gained 54 seats in the House of Representatives and eight seats in the Senate, giving them complete control of Congress.

When FY1995 ended on September 30, 1995, President Clinton and the new Republican controlled Congress, led by House Speaker *Newt Gingrich*, had not yet agreed on a budget. As always when there is a Democratic president in the White House, Republicans want to curtail spending; but never with a Republican president! Anyway, this conflicted with the President Clinton's objectives for education, environment, Medicare, and healthcare. Hence, when Clinton vetoed the Republican spending bill, thus, refusing the Republican budget cuts, House Speaker Gingrich refused to raise the debt ceiling; putting the country in default. The spending bills Republicans presented to President Clinton would also:

- strip the U.S. Treasury of its ability to dip into federal trust funds to avoid a borrowing crisis
- have limited appeals by death-row inmates
- complicate issuing health, safety and environmental regulations
- commit the President to a 7-year budget plan
- allow the government to keep operating beyond the time when spending authority expires
- increase Medicare Part-B premiums/cancel scheduled reduction

As a result, the federal government put non-essential government workers on furlough and suspended non-essential services on November 14th. The budget shutdown concluded six days later on November 19th, with Congress enacting a temporary spending bill, but the underlying disagreement between President Clinton and House Speaker Gingrich was not resolved. President vetoed a second spending bill and the government shut down a second time on December 16th and lasted 21-days, ending on January 6th, 1996.

While the shutdown was still in the midst, New Gingrich voiced a complaint while attending a breakfast hosted by *Lars-Erik Nelson* of the international news organization, *Christian Science Monitor*. Gingrich stated, during a flight to and from the funeral of *Yitzhak Rabin*, the late Prime Minister of Israel, Clinton had not taken the time to discuss the budget and Gingrich had been directed to leave the plane through the rear door. In a room full of Journalists, the perception arose that the government shutdown was partly due to this "snub" by Clinton. The media did not hesitate to reflect this perception, including an editorial cartoon depicting Newt Gingrich as an whining infant throwing a temper tantrum. Democrats then took this opportunity to attack Gingrich's motives for the shutdown. Finally, the polls indicated Gingrich's credibility was now severely damaged. And the political winds shifted in Clinton's favor.

According to independent economists, Newt Gingrich and the 104th Congress did more harm than good when they shut down the government. But this is something Republicans never consider when they are busy throwing their temper tantrums! A 2010 *Congressional Research Service* report revealed other details of the 1995-1996 government shutdowns. The report indicated the shutdown impacted every sector of the economy! Health and welfare services for military veterans were reduced; the Centers for Disease Control and Prevention stopped disease surveillance; new clinical research patients were not accepted at the National Institutes of Health; and toxic waste clean-up work at 609 sites was halted. Other impacts included: the closure of 368 National Park sites resulting in the loss of seven million visitors; 200,000 applications for passports and 20,000 to 30,000 applications for visas by foreigners went unprocessed each day the government was closed; U.S. tourism and airline industries incurred millions of dollars in losses; and more than 20% of federal contracts ($3.7-billion in spending) were adversely affected.

The Republican shutdowns during the Clinton administration are often overlooked as possible contributors to the 2008 collapse of the U.S. economy. To say the least, the shutdowns did weaken an economy that was already on the path to collapsing over the next 12-years. But if actions speak louder than words, Republicans don't care if the U.S. economy collapsed! Remember who they are, historically: Southern Confederate Democrats (masquerading as Republicans) still fighting and trying to win the civil war; but this time through politics!

Forced To Buy Healthcare?

One day, I heard a Rightwing advocate say with the utmost certainty, *"Obamacare is unconstitutional!"* As it turned out, he was just repeating what he heard the night before on Fox News' Sean Hannity. Republican Congresswoman *Michelle Bachmann* was the guest and during the interview she said, *"It is not within out power as members of Congress ... It's not within the enumerated powers of the Constitution for us to design and create a national takeover of healthcare. Nor is it within our ability to delegate that responsibility to the Executive (President)."* They then continued with a Rightwing back and forth off each other's opinions. But it's funny how Republicans never voiced that concern when President Reagan was privatizing healthcare in the 1980's.

As usual, Fox News viewers believe without question what they are told. And then they repeat what they were told as though it is the indubitable truth! But if they bothered to do their own research, they would find the Congresswoman was dead-wrong about the requirements of the Constitution. To be exact, the Preamble of the Constitution states, *"We the People of the United States, in order to form a more perfect Union, establish justice, insure domestic tranquility, provide for the common defense, promote the general welfare (of United States citizens)."* Is the underlined text *"We the people"* to be taken at face-value or is it only referring to the politicians in the room at the time the document was written? Who did all the writing; every U.S. citizen or their representatives? Were the literal people even aware a Constitution was being written?

Immediately following the Preamble is Article I, defining the federal government. In the context in which the text is written, the word *"welfare"* refers to health, happiness, prosperity and well-being. This language supports the idea of a central government making healthcare available to all its citizens. Article I/Section 8 says, *"The Congress shall have power to lay and collect taxes, duties, imposts and excises, to pay the debts and provide for the common defense and general welfare of the United States ..."* Rather than item specific subject matters, such as healthcare (on which Congress is allowed to spend money), the framers chose to give Congress a broad mandate to spend money in ways that promote the general welfare. Does providing healthcare for every U.S. citizen promote the general welfare of the country? Well, if everyone is equally healthy, everyone can equally pursue the American dream! Perhaps, this is an underlying reason Republicans are against the thought of making healthcare available to every U.S. citizen.

A few weeks later, I heard a different version of this same argument. I saw footage of Congresswoman Michele Bachmann on Face The Nation (CBS). Whoever she was challenging (Obama, Romney or both) she said, *"I am firmly against the individual mandate. I think it is unconstitutional, whether it's put into place at the state level by a state legislature or whether it's put into place at the federal level. I think it's unconstitutional."* Like all Rightwing advocates, Ms. Bachmann expressed her personal opinion without providing any supporting date to back it up! Regardless, the Rightwing minions ran around repeating her opinion as though it were fact. Why exactly is the individual mandate, requiring every adult U.S. citizen to buy their own healthcare insurance considered unconstitutional? Ms. Bachmann never provided an explanation.

When I first heard the individual mandate argument I wondered, *"Who, in their right mind, wouldn't want healthcare insurance?"* The more I listened and the more I learned, I realized it was only the Rightwing minions who were so accustomed to taking full advantage of the "free" taxpayer healthcare provided by privatized Reagancare.   In 1986, President Reagan and the 99th Congress passed the *Consolidated Omnibus Budget Reconciliation Act*, which contained the *Emergency Medical Treatment and Active Labor Act*, requiring every hospital that received Medicare funds (practically every hospital in the country at the time) to treat patients in need of emergency care regardless of their ability to pay, citizenship or even legal status. This was also known as the Reagan mandate! Who would foot the bill for all those people? The taxpayers!

In essence, when the Rightwing minions complain about being forced to buy their own healthcare insurance, they are virtually saying, they prefer that the taxpayers buy their healthcare insurance for them! And at the same time, they call President Obama's *Patient Protection and Affordable Care Act (PPACA)* that cancels out the Reagan mandate, Socialism (with a very nasty undertone)! In addition, the Rightwing minions act as though there is no reason for President Obama's individual healthcare mandate. Since the 1986 Reagan mandate providing free taxpayer healthcare at the ER, economists have tracked the costs.

Twenty-two years of data revealed the expense state governments incur when people require medical care after crossing state lines. And technically, anything crossing state lines becomes a federal matter whether it's a crime (i.e. kidnapping, bank robbery) or the average U.S. citizen on vacation! In this latter case, the federal government can insist you buy healthcare insurance in much the same way it insists you wear a seatbelt while driving. In the event you are hurt outside the state you live in, you drain the resources of the state you were hurt in.   In essence, having your own healthcare insurance is much like having your own auto insurance. And in case you don't know, "auto insurance" is also a federal mandate! The federal government requires that everyone who owns a car possess minimal insurance coverage. However, "minimal coverage" varies and is defined by the state you live in.

If, for any reason, you require medical attention while visiting another state, you drain the resources of that state if you don't provide your own insurance coverage. Now, multiply you by millions of other people who travel from state-to-state on a daily basis! Those medical expenses add up if people don't have their own healthcare insurance coverage. And from that perspective, the individual states should support President Obama's individual mandate for healthcare insurance unless they don't mine footing the bill for the thousands of uninsured people from other states.

The Socialist!

In order to learn what Republicans mean when they call the president a Socialist, you must first learn what they mean when they use the word, "Socialism". Initially, the Rightwing minions learn the evils historically associated with Adolf Hitler's National Socialist Party. In German it's "**Na**tionals**o**z**i**alistische", shortened to "Nazi". Rightwing minions then suggest Nazis were "Socialists" in general. On the contrary, it's full name, the *National Socialist German Workers' Party* evolved from the German nationalist, racist and populist Freikorps paramilitary culture, that fought against communist uprisings in post-World War I Germany.

German nationalist suggested they believed in the unity of the German people as a race (or master race) in Europe. Hence, the racist element that segregated and ranked the different European races and the various segments of German citizens. But at the same time, it was "populist" believing a political system that favors the people instead of the wealthy elites. But I suppose "the people" can be exclusive to the German people. And finally, Freikorps comprised a German volunteer military. So, they did believed in bringing change through hostilities and violence.

For the record, the country of Sweden is Socialist; it has a Socialist government! And if it wasn't for the winter Olympics, the world would not hear a peep out of them! In comparison, Adolf Hitler's

National Socialists (Nazis) were hostile, destructive, loud, rude, and they started the second world war! They were not socialists (equality for all), they were fascists (dictators)! Hence, Socialists and National Socialists are two entirely different thing! In essence, they are complete opposites!

To take this propaganda a step further, Rightwing advocates claim "Socialized Medicine" is a subtle way to introduce "Socialism (i.e. Adolf Hitler's National Socialist Party/Nazism)" into American society. When he was an actor, Ronald Reagan made a verbal recording (record) of the evils of socialized medicine. In it he said, *"One of the traditional methods of imposing statism or socialism on a people has been by way of medicine ... It's very easy to disguise a medical program as a humanitarian project, most people are a little reluctant to oppose anything that suggests medical care for people who possibly can't afford it ... and one day we will awake to find, we have Socialism!"* Hence, they suggest the "Socialized" in *Socialized Medicine* is the same as the "Socialist" in *National Socialist*, concluding "Socialism" is a very bad thing! Even though to name a few, Socialized Medicine:

- invented the Pacemaker
- discovered insulin for Diabetes
- the first to practice Chemotherapy on cancer patients
- the first to practice Heart Surgery by a robot
- invented the Electric Wheelchair
- discovered the DNA gene for Cystic Fibrosis
- the first to use a robot to reduce strokes in a common cardiac disorder
- the first to use an Artificial Kidney machine
- discovered the Chemotherapy drugs Vinca Alkaloids
- the first Liver transplant
- the first to finish the Human Genome map
- the first robotic-assisted Left Atrial Appendage Ligation for stroke prevention

Rightwing advocates go through all this trouble to demonize the idea of "Socialized Medicine" because Republican politicians (and their Rightwing lobbyists) prefer the idea of "privatization". What's the difference?

MULTI-MILLION DOLLAR PRIVATE INSURANCE COMPANIES
- set rates (normally high monthly premiums)
- make the policies
- make the rules
- make the regulations
- set the criteria for coverage
- set astronomical costs for operations
- affordability is out the window

In other words, the private insurance companies stack-the-deck to "they" profit and "you" spend the rest of your life paying off the astronomical medical bills they made sure you have!

In addition to that, Republicans cover-up the fact that privatized healthcare is unconstitutional! As stated in the Preamble, *"We the people of the United States, in order to form a more perfect union ... 'promote the general welfare' ..."* not "privatize" the general welfare! In essence, as much as Republicans give the impression letting the insurance companies control healthcare (privatization) is much better than letting the government control healthcare (socialism), the Constitution tells us the health of every U.S. citizen (the general welfare) is the responsibility of the government. And private insurance companies do not have every U.S. citizen's best interests in mind. On the contrary, they are only concerned about their own "profit margins". And typically, this excludes millions of U.S. citizens insurance companies could care less about!

The Rightwing minions are conditioned to zero-in on the downside of socialized medicine as though privatization does not have a downside of its own. If you have enough money (or the right insurance), you can get better quality medical attention a lot faster! Need an MRI? Just cough over $5,000 by any means necessary and "BAM" you're getting an MRI done! That's privatization baby! But what about the millions of people who cannot come up with $5,000 in an instant? You don't get an MRI, ever! So, for people with large incomes, privatization is great! But the vast majority of incomes (and insurance) are not that great under a privatized system! While the Rightwing minions zero-in on the downside of socialized medicine, they zero-in on the upside of privatization.

The Rightwing minions never tell the complete story of privatized healthcare. During the 1980s on into the new century, getting sick and going to the hospital was expensive. When people needed medical attention, the healthcare costs were either paid out of pocket or through insurance. Even people who were lucky enough to have health coverage didn't walk away without incurring debt. Insurance policies (rigged in favor of the companies that provided them) usually required a co-payment of 20%. This forced millions of middle-class people to delay seeking treatment in the hope that their symptoms would subside. If not, it usually meant a trip to the emergency room because the disease or injury had progressed to the point that the trip became necessary. And President Reagan made sure hospitals could not turn away emergency cases!

And let's not forget about all those silly, unrealistic rules insurance companies came up with to insure "you" got stuck with a high medical bill. But eventually, insurance companies developed the managed-care concept to control the astronomical costs of medical treatment. Under managed-care, people could seek treatment without being stuck with a bill afterward. Unfortunately, the catch was "costly insurance premiums" in addition to the extremely rigid and often ridiculous set of rules you had to follow. If a rule was broken (for any reason, unavoidable or otherwise), you got stuck with a medical bill that took years to pay off! The privatization lie is that a healthcare system that can pursue the dual goals of providing optimum care and making insane profits will somehow improve services and reduce costs!

The Rightwing minions claim the Harry Truman administration proposed a compulsory health insurance program for all people in the United States and the American people unhesitatingly rejected the idea! Let the Rightwing minions tell the story, that was all there was to it! As always, they leave out everything Republicans and Rightwing advocates did to create fear and panic in the minds of millions of Americans to get them to reject the Truman proposal. Even the *American Medical Association* (AMA) launched a spirited attack against capitalizing on fears of Communism in the public mind that existed at the time. The AMA characterized Truman's health proposals as "socialized medicine" and called Truman White House staffers "followers of the Moscow party line".

For the record, the AMA is to healthcare as the NRA (National Rifle Association) is to gun control. It has one of the largest political lobbying budgets of any organization in the United States. The political positions throughout the AMA's history has often been on the side of controversy. For instance, in the 1930s, the AMA attempted to prohibit its members from working for the then-primitive health maintenance organizations that sprung up during the Great Depression. This violated the Sherman Antitrust (Anti-Competition) Act and resulted in a conviction ultimately affirmed by the Supreme Court. In the 1950's, the AMA vehement campaigned against Medicare and 1960's endorsed *Operation Coffee Cup* (the record Ronald Reagan recorded demonizing socialized medicine that would be played during thousands of coffee meetings) in opposition to Democratic plans to extend Social Security to include health insurance for the elderly (i.e. Medicare).

While we're on the subject, the term "*socialized medicine*" was first used by the AMA in 1917 as a "positive epithet" that praised the following achievements:
- discovering disease in its incipiency;
- helping to end venereal diseases, alcoholism, tuberculosis;
- making a major contribution to social welfare

But by the 1930s, "socialized medicine" was regularly used as a negative epithet by Rightwing opponents who supported privatized healthcare and opposed publicly funded healthcare, implying it represented socialism (and by extension, communism). In 1947, in an effort to ridicule President Truman's proposal for a national healthcare system, the AMA hired the public relations firm Whitaker & Baxter to spearhead a smear campaign that demonized Truman's efforts. In doing so, they popularized "socialized medicine" as a "negative epithet" that demonized anyone who supported the idea of publicly funded healthcare as a communist! This method preyed on the fears the general public harbored towards communism.

During the 2008 campaign season, Rightwing advocates revamped the term to conform to their distorted interpretation of socialism. The term "Obamacare" emerged as another epithet dreamt up by Rightwing advocates to suggest "universal healthcare" or "socialized medicine" was invented by President Obama, The Evil Socialist! I suppose in the imaginary world they live in, this is a very bad thing! But I think "Obamacare" actually resonates with a lot of people in a good way. Howbeit, unintentionally!

Before I move on, I want to address a challenge a Rightwing advocate targeting my assessment of all these documented facts stating, *"Insulin was discovered by Dr. Frederick Banting in 1922; Universal Healthcare was not in Canada until 1946."* My retort? First of all, *"universal healthcare"* and *"socialized medicine"* are two entirely different things. The former (universal healthcare) refers to the actual system which provides healthcare and financial protection to all its citizens. The latter (socialized medicine) can mean just about anything! Do not assume the party who uses the term "socialized medicine" means "universal healthcare". They can mean "socialism", "communism", or "you're evil". And for the record, Frederick Banting, Charles Best, J.J.R. Macleod, and James Collip did the research at the University of Toronto, funded by the Canadian government!

The Community Organizer

The Rightwing minions are programmed to routinely call President Obama a "*Community Organizer* (with a nasty undertone)". What exactly do they have against community organizers and the work they do for local communities? Once Rightwing advocates convince themselves community organizing is a bad thing, they attack without mercy! What they don't seem to realize is rational people appreciate community organizers and the work they do. In addition, there is a very good possibility the Rightwing minions who demonize the president as a community organizer has benefited from community organizing most of their lives.

I was half-watching the 2008 Republican Convention when I heard vice-presidential pick Sarah Palin poke fun at Democrat Barack Obama's experience as a community organizer. This got my full attention, I raised one eye-brow with a question mark over head. Why is she belittling community organizing? Although, it is the method in which people who feel disenfranchised respond to out-of-touch politicians and their failed policies, it was quite obvious the audience immediately picked up on the subliminal message, *"community organizing is a bad thing!"* More specifically, a young Barack Obama moved to Chicago (after he finished college) and got involved with church-based organizing to help people who lost their jobs due to the massive lay-offs and manufacturing plant closings in southeast Chicago.

With this in mind, Sarah Palin devalued Barack Obama's noble community organizing efforts in response to her Democratic critics challenging her own experience as the Mayor of Wasilla (a small city in Alaska with a population of about 5,000 at the time) from 1996 to 2002. However, the voting base of Wasilla was not more than 1,500 registered voters. Palin won the mayoral race defeating the incumbent *John Stein* by a vote of 651 to 440. Democrats begged to question whether or not Sarah Palin would ever have won a mayoral race in a much larger city with thousands of voters. As a result, Palin compared her humble beginnings as the mayor of Wasilla, Alaska to Obama's humble beginnings as a community organizer. And in doing so, claimed community organizing did not require any real responsibility. But let's examine that assessment!

In 1985, *Jerry Kellman* (head of the *Calumet Community Religious Conference;* a Catholic social justice group based on the south side of Chicago/northern Indiana), hired Obama as the first director of their new branch, *Developing Communities Project*. Obama's job description: find out what the people needed (i.e. job training programs, asbestos removal, potholes filled, traffic signs posted) and teach them how to work together to get action from their elected officials. At the time, Chicago's south side was devastated by factory closings and pollution; and the people were discouraged by poverty and discrimination. In addition to convincing down trodden workers to try again, Obama had to teach them to work with people they didn't quite see eye to eye with. In doing so, he interviewed them, helped them strategize, and taught them how to use the natural gifts they possessed. This experience turned out to be the model for his highly successful presidential campaign.

As it turned out, Sarah Palin thought Barack Obama's community organizing experience was a joke until election day! In protest to

Palin's attack on community organizers, I saw a person wearing a tee-shirt that read, "Jesus was a community organizer and Pontius Pilate was a Governor". I immediately knew this referred to Sarah Palin, former Governor of Alaska, and the remarks she made about Barack Obama's history as a community organizer. But be that all as it may, another detail that was still pressing in the back of my mind regarded why Sarah Palin, the Republican vice-presidential challenger, compared herself to Barack Obama, the presidential challenger. Shouldn't she be comparing her history with that of Joe Biden, the Democratic incumbent vice-president? Throughout the entire 2008 presidential campaign, Rightwing minions continued to compare Sarah Palin's political experience to that of Barack Obama.

This brings up another thing I noticed about Rightwing advocates; they always compare apples and watermelons to make a point! Sarah Palin was running for the office of vice-president but constantly compared herself to Barack Obama, who was running for a different office. Palin's attacks should have been directed at her opponent, Joe Biden! But that detail aside, Palin compared Obama's very first job fresh out of college (making an annual salary of $10,000) to the third position she held in politics! Her first political victory was on the Wasilla City Council in 1992 (against telephone company worker, *John Hartrick*); she won by a 530 to 310 victory. In 1995, she won her re-election bid against *R'nita Rogers* in a 410 to 185 vote victory.

But if you want to compare apples to apples, immediately after her college graduation, Sarah Palin became a sportscaster! Another interesting detail about Palin's academic history; she spent 5-years and six colleges to get a Bachelor's degree:

- 1982 - University of Hawaii, Hilo
- 1982 - Hawaii Pacific University, Honolulu
- 1983 - North Idaho College, Coeur d'Alene
- 1984 - University of Idaho, Moscow
- 1985 - Matanuska-Susitna College, Alaska
- 1986 - University of Idaho, Moscow

At the end of her academic trek, Palin excelled in Communications-Journalism. After graduation, she worked as a sportscaster for KTUU-TV and KTVA-TV in Anchorage, then a sports reporter for the

Mat-Su Valley Frontiersman. It was because of this popularity, she won small town elections to the Wasilla City Council and Mayor. In addition, she became a registered Republican in 1982 and had the financial backing of the Republican Party, even though the Wasilla Mayor's races was non-partisan (neither Republican or Democrat).

While we're still on the subject, I recall an earlier John McCain interview on NBC's Nightly News shortly after he announced "Sarah Palin" as his vice-presidential pick. When questioned about her experience relative to becoming the next vice-president of the United States, McCain included Palin's involvement with PTA as one of the examples of her executive experience. The PTA? The Parent-Teacher Association? Now, don't get me wrong. I'm not knocking anyone who works on the PTA. I'm sure that involves a lot of hard work and dedication. Especially, since most (if not everyone) involved work on a volunteer basis. But the only critique I have is the fact that the PTA falls under community organizing! Now, why is community organizing a good thing when it's Sarah Palin and a bad thing when it's Barack Obama?

The Food Stamp President

By now, you've probably heard Rightwing advocates refer to President Obama as *"The Food Stamp President."* The minions got this from presidential hopeful Newt Gingrich. In an effort to distinguish himself from the other presidential GOP candidates (during the 2012 Republican Primaries), Gingrich started pushing the line, *"Obama is the food stamp president."* This accusation to me was intriguing. But unlike the Rightwing minions, I do my own investigations to find out how true a thing is ... or is not!

On first glance, the raw numbers appear to support Gingrich's claim. In early 2008 (during the George W. Bush administration), a record number of Americans were receiving food stamps; 46-million recipients in 22-million households. But this was primarily because of the increased numbers of Americans who suddenly found themselves living below or just hovering above the poverty line because their jobs were outsourced and they became victims of downsizing during the 2008 Recession. This had nothing to do with steps made by the Obama administration to make it easier for non-qualified people to receive food stamps, as Gingrich suggested.

Eligibility for the Supplemental Nutrition Assistance Program (food stamps) depends on household income, assets, childcare, housing and work-related expenses. In fiscal year 2010, according to the U.S. Agriculture Department, about 85% of all households receiving food stamps were under the poverty line, as poverty was rising to record levels. Howbeit unintentionally, Gingrich's comment ignited some backlash; at the time of the comment, 34% of food stamp recipients were white people. And for the record, I know you're wondering, 22% were African-American, 17% Hispanic, 7% Asian or Native American, and 20% race unknown.

For the record, food-stamp use had increased 46% by December of 2008; one month before Barack Obama's inauguration (in January 2009)! Hence, the increasing demand for food stamps actually began during the George W. Bush administration. Prior to its end, the economy was shedding millions of jobs and not everyone survived on the level of finding another job. Millions of new recipients signed up for food stamps among other government assistance programs.

Rightwing minions are always quick to claim other groups dominate government welfare programs. They see themselves as the only demographic that is hardworking. According to the Tax Foundation and the 2012 Census, the top ten Welfare recipient states are:

1) **New Mexico** (Purple/Swing State)
2) **Mississippi** (Republican)
3) **Alaska** (Republican)
4) **Louisiana** (Republican)
5) **West Virginia** (Republican)
6) **Alabama** (Republican)
7) **South Dakota** (Republican)
8) **Kentucky** (Republican)
9) **Virginia** (Republican)
10) **Montana** (Republican)

According to the Department of Agriculture's Food and Nutrition Service, January 2001 through December 2008 (during the George W. Bush Administration), the number of food stamp recipients rose by 14.7-million. As a matter of fact, the Bush administration called food stamps "Nutritional Aid" after millions of newly unemployed White people began to apply for them. No other president's administration before 2001 came anywhere close to this level of increase. Although, from 2009 to 2012, the increase so far has been 14.2-million, this is not the result of anything the Obama administration has done, policy-wise. On the contrary, it is the result of the Obama administration not able to plug the leak that began during the previous George W. Bush administration.

Rightwing advocates appear to have double-vision; they see one increase of 14.7-million food stamp recipients during the George W. Bush administration and a separate increase of 14.2-million during the Barack Obama administration. In other words, they think the rise in food stamp usage "slammed on breaks" when George W. Bush left the White House, reset, and started up again after Barack Obama's inauguration. The fact of the matter is the entire 28.9-million food stamp recipient increase is the result of the George W. Bush administration. Rational people realize the rise in food stamp recipients did not take a break between presidents but rather continued from one administration into the next administration.

While testifying before a House Committee in 2008, economist *Mark Zandi* advised, the best way for stimulating the economy was by increasing food stamp payments and extending unemployment benefits. President Bush then went out of his way to provide food stamps; a.k.a. Bush Bucks! According to the Congressional Budget Office estimates, every $1 paid out in food stamps generates $1.73 of economic activity; every $1 paid out in unemployment benefits generates $1.64 of economic activity. In contrast, every $1 paid out in tax cuts generates $0.29 of economic activity. The experts always say, *"Tax cuts do not pay for themselves!"* These statistics are the driving force behind the reasons Republicans demonize food stamps and refuse to extend unemployment benefits! These will only help to improve the economy; something Republicans don't want to happen during the Obama administration!

The Teleprompter-In-Chief

The teleprompter was invented in 1950 primarily to assist actors who had to learn large amounts of script in a short amount of time. It is mainly a display device that prompts the person speaking with an electronic visual text of a speech/script. Using a teleprompter is similar to the practice of using cue cards. The screen is in front of and usually below the camera lens. The words on the screen are reflected to the eyes of the presenter using a sheet of clear glass or specially prepared beam splitter. Light from the performer passes through the front side of the glass into the lens, while a shroud surrounding the lens and the back side of the glass prevents unwanted light from reflecting into the lens. Whew!

How often do Rightwing advocates criticize President Obama for using a teleprompter? Gee. For people who never watch the man give a speech, they sure seem to know what goes on. Like every other person on TV, maybe the President has used a teleprompter. Be that as it may, what's the problem? The Rightwing minions act as though Barack Obama is the only person in politics who has ever used a teleprompter. On one occasion, Sarah Palin criticized President Obama for using the teleprompter as the media noticed the footnotes written in the palm of her hand. And on a more recent occasion, Palin advised President Obama to do his job and step away from the teleprompter ... as "she" was reading from a teleprompter. It never fails to amaze me how hypocritical the people on the right side of the aisle blatantly are.

And speaking of Rightwing advocates and teleprompters, George W. Bush was obviously dependent on them. I watched some of his speeches and you can see him practically draped over the podium, squinting to read the screen. My god, why didn't he just wear glasses or something? I know he was often teased about not being the smartest guy, but watching this man almost kill himself trying to read the teleprompter didn't help my case of giving him the benefit-of-doubt. Could this be the underlying reason Rightwing advocates keep assaulting President Obama and his alleged teleprompter use?

Since its invention in 1950, the teleprompter has been used by presidents and presidential candidates, Republicans and Democrats alike, seeking precision and accuracy in their speeches.   As a matter of fact, in 1952, Republican President Herbert Hoover was the first politician to ever use a teleprompter; he addressed the Republican National Convention in Chicago with this new marvel in technology. Regardless of the history Republican politicians have had with the teleprompter, they keep taking jabs at President Obama as though he is the only politician to ever use one; as they insinuate Republican politicians never use the teleprompter.

In President Obama's defense, several Republican politicians have been noticed using teleprompters during the 2012 GOP Primary and on other occasions.   Let's see, there was Mitt Romney, Rick Santorum, Ron Paul, Newt Gingrich, John Boehner, Paul Ryan, Rick Perry, Michelle Bachmann, Marco Rubio, Eric Cantor, Jon Huntsman, Herman Cain, Mike Huckabee and Sarah Palin.   Yes. Sarah Palin! On top of that, pictures were taken of all of them that included the unavoidable teleprompter.   But in the long run, the Republican war on teleprompters has poetically backfired. It began as a quasi-racist meme passed from one person to another among the Rightwing minions. It was their way of convincing themselves President Obama was a mindless puppet. But by catering to it, Republican politicians have backed themselves into a position where they themselves cannot benefit from using teleprompters.

It has been said among journalists, Republican politicians are not the most eloquent speakers and not using teleprompters makes them a lot worse than the need to be.   On the upside, the Rightwing audience typically does not require much to stimulate their brain.   Republican politicians can get away with giving a speech comprised of extemporaneous remarks (this means, not planned or rehearsed) comprised of flat out lies and half-truths. This is what they call "winging it". Excellent examples: When Newt Gingrich called President Obama the *"food stamp president"* with no statistical data to back it up! When Sarah Palin called President Obama the *"community organizer"* suggesting it is only a title that requires no time, effort or energy; and not statistical data to back it up!   And now when Sarah Palin criticized President Obama for using a *teleprompter* without pointing out any problem it caused.

Now, with all that said and done, the way I see it, the Rightwing minions are not that bright. From what I've heard, they don't fully understand the use of teleprompters. They suggest, some mysterious puppet master is behind the scenes writing down words the President is suppose to say in front of the camera. Although, this might've been true with George W. Bush, it isn't true for the vast majority of presidents who used teleprompters to win over the country. For instance, Republican President Ronald Reagan was a most excellent user of the teleprompter and nobody complained. The teleprompter is not about making the President (or any other presenter) a puppet. In politics, it's primarily about speechwriters. Now, if the Rightwing advocates have a more specific problem with speechwriters, they should fess-up! U.S. Presidents have used speechwriters for the last 50(+) years and nobody complained.

President Obama has never kept the fact he uses a speechwriter a secret. And for the record, speechwriters don't dream up what they want the president to say, they take the president's own words and ideas and put them in the best words possible for clarity's sake. So, if President Obama uses a teleprompter, the screen is displaying his own words but written more eloquently by a professional. That's why President Obama is known for giving great speeches; he has the best speechwriter in the business!

On the other hand, the Republican Party is single-minded on the issues provided by the Heritage Foundation; a Rightwing think tank (based in Washington, D.C.) that formulates and promotes *free enterprise* (no government regulations preventing business, banks and wall street from profiting by any means necessary; no consumer protection laws that protect the public from unscrupulous business and bank practices; the very same practices that led to the 1929 Stock Market crash, 1930s Great Depression, and 2008 Recession), *limited government* (each state should be like an independent country government by a wealthy minority; federal level used to enforce "religious views (bigotry, racism, discrimination)" that keep the wealthy minorities in power, *individual freedom* (the Rightwing minions are free to commit acts of terror when it suits them (like the recent George Washington Bridge incident in New Jersey), *traditional American values* (bigotry, racism, prejudice, hate, Jim Crow laws), a strong national defense (attack other countries first, before they attack us)!

It is no big secret where Republicans stand (or are told to stand by the Heritage Foundation) on any given issue:

- gun control (everyone should own a gun)
- tax breaks for the rich (tax burden the middle-class)
- cutting spending (for the poor and middle-class; not for the rich)
- healthcare (privatization baby!)
- gay marriage (less federal money for private corporations)
- abortion (less federal money for private corporations)
- immigration (less federal money for private corporations)

It never really matters which Republican candidate wins a GOP Primary during a presidential election year. They will all stick to the script provided to them by the Heritage Foundation and the rich and powerful tycoons who want to manipulate all the laws, rules, regulations, and guidelines to exclusively benefit THEM under the guise of Rightwing philosophy!

Laissez-Faire

The Republican Party adopted the philosophy, Laissez-faire. This is a French term that means, *"let [them] do"* but broadly implies *"let it be"* or *"leave it alone."* In practice, Laissez-faire is an economic environment in which transactions between private parties are free from tariffs, government subsidies and enforced monopolies, with only enough government regulations to protect property rights against theft and aggression. Hence, enforcing this philosophy keeps government regulations out of private enterprise; which is free to do whatever they can dream up to profit. This normally includes figuring out ways to take complete advantage of millions of unsuspecting consumers. Republicans never mention the fact the government regulations they so desperately want to get rid of includes all the consumer protection laws, as well!

The Republican Party strives to have a federal government that intervenes as little as possible in economic affairs. Put another way, your life should be dictated by private corporations instead of the federal government! At least, that is what it all boils down to;

who gets to tell you how to live. This is one of the main reasons, the Heritage Foundation works overtime to get its Rightwing minions to hate the idea of the federal government telling them what they can or cannot do. In 2009, the Rightwing minions made a big stink about the individual healthcare mandate that, according to them, forces them to buy healthcare insurance.

In the 1980s, President Ronald Reagan was very instrumental in severing federal government regulations from private enterprise. He often referred to the process as *"getting the government off the back of the business."* As much as we'd all love to love "The Gipper", he was not the economic genius the Rightwing minions suggest he was.   Ronald Reagan followed the same Rightwing agenda as every other Republican president since 1921. Ergo, they want to create a world where a 10% wealthy minority owns and controls everything, with a 10% middle-class buffer between them and the 80% masses who live in poverty. But look at the bright side, they won't force you to buy healthcare insurance because they don't want you to have healthcare insurance.   This is the Republican idea of individual freedom!

According to Right philosophy, private corporations are created to do one thing; make money. And if a company isn't making money it will cease to exist in the near future.   Hence, companies are pressured to make money by any means necessary. The Rightwing minions insist government intervention makes it harder for private enterprise to make money. The truth of the matter is government intervention makes it harder for private enterprise to "cheat consumers" in order to make money! Hence, what the Rightwing advocates refrain from saying is Republicans want to get rid of "government regulations" so private enterprise can make as much money as they possibly can by cheating unsuspecting consumers! On top of this, after they make astronomical amounts of money from cheating unsuspecting consumers, they want tax breaks! Hence, they also want the consumers they cheat on a daily bases to pay the lion's share of the federal tax burden!

Thus, The Republican Party of Corporations work tirelessly to get taxes, regulations (or the lack thereof) and economic policies to benefit the rich and private corporations. Let me specify the fact that private corporations are "legal entities". Mitt Romney was correct when he stated, *"corporations are people"*. A corporation can legally do just about anything a person can do. Corporations can vote, pay taxes, get tax breaks, rent, lease, own, purchase, make money, save, invest, have bank accounts, trusts, apply for loans, repay loans and file for bankruptcy. It is customary for rich people to own corporations that owns their riches. This way, the corporation is not held liable for any law suits, liens, or personal debts the owner might have. Hence, their money is untouchable!

In analogy, Republicans are like a football team that wants to play the game without having to follow the rules, regulations, referees, or respect the government who provided the stadium and the playing field, and want to keep all the money from the ticket sales without giving anything back to the stadium or the fans. Rightwing advocates think they are entitled to just show up and have everything handed to them without having to obey any rules or play the game on a level playing field.

You Didn't Build That?
On July 13, 2012, President Obama delivered a speak in Roanoke, Virginia, where he made a remark in the context of his belief that wealthy citizens should pay higher taxes:

There are a lot of wealthy, successful Americans who agree with me - because they want to give something back. They know they didn't - look, if you've been successful, you didn't get there on your own. If you were successful, somebody along the line gave you some help. There was a great teacher somewhere in your life. Somebody helped to create this unbelievable American system that we have that allowed you to thrive. Somebody invested in roads and bridges. If you've got a business - **you didn't build that**. Somebody else made that happen.

And the Rightwing minions extrapolated four words from President Obama's speech, *"you didn't build that"*, and quoted it out-of-context as thought that's the only thing he said, *"You didn't build that!"* Hence, another Rightwing philosophy is that they build their businesses with no help from the federal government. And it's not the federal government they come crying to every time they need billions of dollars worth of taxpayer funded bailouts to rescue them from the financial ruins of their own deregulation creation. And oil companies, insurance companies and farmers don't count on billions of dollars worth of federal subsidies, ever! And private banks don't count of the federal government insuring every dollar their customers deposit. And private corporations don't depend on the "corporate status" and "tax breaks" provided to them by the federal government they're mocking.

Of course, all of that was sarcasm, for the opposite is true. All those Rightwing advocates who claim they did it all by themselves, are choosing to live in a delusional world where the help they got from the federal government is non-existent. Yeah. Not one of them ever got a federally funded start-up loan to help their business get off the ground. They forget all about that the moment their business can stand on its own two feet! All President Obama said was, "You didn't do that on your own. Acknowledge the help you received along the way!" The delusional Rightwing minions refuse to thank the teachers who taught them how to read, write and count. They would much rather see teachers lose all their salaries, benefits and bargaining rights!

Political Satire

RIGHTWING ADVOCATE: I built this business WITHOUT any help from the federal government!

FEDERAL GOV: Duhr uhm ... While you were so busy building your business, we provided:

- Your Trademark Name (so no one else can use it)
- The Ports where Cargo ships dock that import the goods you sell
- Reliable electricity policies so you don't have to work in the dark
- Fair electric rates so you don't have to work out of a cave
- Fair access to electricity so you and your competitors have an even chance of success
- Fair access to radio waves so you can listen to the radio
- Fair access to telephones so you can communicate nationwide
- Inspections of all those delicious delicacies that you enjoy eating to make them safe for your consumption
- Tracking and annihilating diseases and outbreaks that could kill you and your family
- Standard currency for the transaction of your goods

- The Fire Department down the street in the event you work so hard, you're careless
- The Police Department up the road in the event you become the victim of a crime
- Regulate air traffic so you can fly anywhere in the country, safely
- Trade Agreements for the import of basic goods, like the cloths you're wearing
- Standard Date and Time, so you can stay on schedule
- The property drainage all around your business so it is not flooded during heavy rains
- Driving standards so it is safe for you to get from home to work
- The roads between your home and your business or where ever else you need to drive
- Postal Service so you can send and receive parcels or even have mail order items
- Public Education so you can read, write, count and some day get a job or create one
- Fought and won all the wars that threatened our way of life
- Fighting terrorism to keep our land safe
- The Internet, so you can get online and claim how much you don't need the federal government

> *"Under a separation of state and economics, especially with <u>laissez-faire capitalism</u> [Free Trade], the state no longer has a role to play in protecting the people and assuring their happiness. Laissez-faire means capitalism is outside the regulatory control of the state and that the people are entirely at the mercy of the capitalists."*
> *-**Thomas Jefferson**-*

> *"I see in the near future a crisis approaching that unnerves me and causes me to tremble for the safety of my country ... Corporations have been enthroned and an era of corruption in high places will follow, and the money power of the country will endeavor to prolong its reign by working upon the prejudices of the people until all wealth is aggregated in a few hands and the Republic is destroyed."*
> *-**Abraham Lincoln**-*

Smaller Government

I have noticed over, the moment there is a Democrat living in the White House, Republicans start screaming for smaller government! I suppose when there is a Republican living in the White House, we are to assume the federal government is much smaller in size. I took it upon myself to put this assumption to the test. I went as far back as the Gerald Ford [R] administration. According to the Federal Employment Statistics published by the Office of Personnel Management, on December 31, 1976 (towards the end of the Ford administration), the total nonmilitary personnel count of federal employees was **2,883,000**. In comparison, on December 31, 1980 (towards the end of the Jimmy Carter [D] administration), the total nonmilitary employee count was **2,875,000**. Hence, the federal nonmilitary employee count was reduced by **8,000** under the Democratic Carter Administration.

Further research reveal, on January 21, 1981, the Ronald Reagan [R] administration began with **2,875,000** nonmilitary federal employees from the previous Carter administration. By the end of Reagan's second term the total number of nonmilitary federal employees had increased to **3,113,000**. Hence, during the Reagan administration, the nonmilitary federal employee count increased by **238,000**.

On January 20, 1989, the George H.W. Bush [R] administration began with a total nonmilitary employee count of **3,113,000** from the previous Reagan administration. By the end of his only term, this Bush administration had actually reduced to **3,083,000** federal nonmilitary employees. Ergo, this Republican president reduced the Reagan's nonmilitary federal employ count by **30,000**. This is the first (and last) time Republicans can claim they actually reduced the size of the federal government. And not from a previous president who was a Democrat, I might add.

In 1993, the Bill Clinton [D] administration began with **3,083,000** from the previous George H.W. Bush Administration. By 2001 (the end of his second term), Clinton reduced the number of federal employees to **2,703,000**; a reduction of **380,000**. Does this suggest the previous George H.W. Administration could've reduced the size of government by **410,000** employees?

In 2001, the George W. Bush [R] administration began with **2,703,000** nonmilitary employees from the previous Bill Clinton administration. By 2008, the total nonmilitary federal employee count was **2,756,000**. This Bush administration increased the size of the federal government by **53,000** employees.

Finally, in 2009, the Barack Obama [D] administration began with **2,756,000** nonmilitary federal employees from the previous Bush Administration. By the end of 2009, the nonmilitary federal employee count was **2,748,978**. Hence, he lowered nonmilitary federal employees by **7,022** fewer than the previous Bush administration. However, by the end of 2010, the count of federal nonmilitary employees increased to **2,840,000**. In other words, the count increased by **91,022** employees.

As much as Republicans don't want to admit it, the Obama administration is an exception to the rule; it began with the 2008 Recession. Hence, treating it the same as previous administrations is not an accurate comparison. It is understandable the Obama administration needed to spend money and hire new employees to combat the housing market collapse, the banking industry collapse, the stock market collapse, the auto industry collapse, and stop the sky from collapsing on all our heads. Be that as it may, the Obama administration still has fewer nonmilitary federal employees than the Reagan administration did in a booming economy. This is also considering the fact the population has grown from 226,545,805 to approximately 315,000,000.

Big Government Spending

Another Republican deception emerges from the words "STOP THE SPENDING!" whenever there is a Democrat living in the White House. The suggestion is when in power, Democrats spend more than Republicans! Once again, I did my own research to put this claim to the test. To my shocking surprise, I discovered President Barack Obama is the smallest government spender since President Dwight D. Eisenhower [R] of the 1950s! And President Obama managed to do this with a much larger population and in the midst of a recession. According to MarketWatch.com, of all the falsehoods Republicans tell about President Obama, the biggest whopper is the one about his reckless spending spree. Although there was a big stimulus bill under Obama in 2009, federal spending is rising at the slowest pace since Dwight Eisenhower brought the Korean War to an end in the 1950s. As a matter of fact, during the Great Depression, President Herbert Hoover [R] (1929-1933) increased spending more than President Obama has.

According to the records at the Office of Management and Budget, in the FY2009 (the last budget under George W. Bush), federal spending rose by 17.9% from $2.98-trillion to $3.52-trillion. In FY2010 (the first budget under President Obama), spending fell 1.8% to $3.46-trillion. However, in FY2011, spending rose 4.3% to $3.60-trillion. And according to the Congressional Budget Office's estimate of the budget that was agreed to in August 2011, in FY2012, spending was set rise 0.7% to $3.63-trillion. Finally, in FY2013 (the final budget of President Obama's first term), spending was scheduled to fall 1.3% to $3.58-trillion.

Over President Obama's four budget years, federal spending is on track to rise from $3.52-trillion to $3.58-trillion, an annualized increase of just 0.4%. Despite what you may have heard from the Rightwing minion's gossip, there has been no huge increase in spending under Obama; Rightwing minions have a very basic misunderstanding of the federal budget. And that's giving them the benefit-of-doubt; I could just call them stupid! The Rightwing minions don't consider the fact the first year of every presidential term starts with a budget approved by the previous administration. Hence, the Obama administration began with the last budget set by the previous George W. Bush administration. The president only begins to shape the budget in his second year in office.

It takes time to develop a budget and steer it through Congress; especially in these days of congressional gridlock. Thus, the FY2009 budget, that Rightwing minions include as part of President Obama's legacy, actually began 4-months before his inauguration. The major spending decisions in the FY2009 budget were made by George W. Bush and the previous Congress; which for the record was controlled by the Democrats. But technically, what could a

Democratic controlled Congress really do in the last year of a Republican president if they disapprove of his budget? Shut down the government just one month before the presidential general election? First off, shutting down the government is a Republican ploy. And second, such an action would provide Republicans with enough ammunition that would guarantee the next the Democratic candidate would lose the presidential election.

Like a relief pitcher who comes into the game with the bases loaded, President Obama came in with a budget in place (set by the previous administration) that called for spending to increase by hundreds of billions of dollars in response to the worst economic and financial calamity since the Great Depression of the 1930s! And according to all the records out there, Republicans have always been the big government spenders they claim Democrats are. As a matter of documented fact, the Republican Party invented "corporate bailouts" for businesses "to big to fail". The following is track record of bailouts handed out by Republican presidents:

1970, **Richard Nixon**, $3.2-Billion Bailout
1971, **Richard Nixon**, $1.4-Billion Bailout
1974, **Gerald Ford**, $7.8-Billion Bailout
1975, **Gerald Ford**, $9.4-Billion Bailout
1981, **Ronald Reagan**, $4-Billion Bailout
1984, **Ronald Reagan**, $9.5-Billion Bailout
1989, **George H. W. Bush**, $293-Billion Bailout
2001, **George W. Bush**, $18.6-Billion Bailout
2008, **George W. Bush**, $30-Billion Bailout
2008 **George W. Bush**, $400-Billion Bailout
2008 **George W. Bush**, $180-Billion Bailout
2008 **George W. Bush**, $25-Billion Bailout
2008 **George W. Bush**, $700-Billion Bailout
2008 **George W. Bush**, $280-Billion Bailout
2009, **George W. Bush**, $142.2 Billion Bailout

These mega-billions kept various private banks, railway companies, auto companies and airlines from failing. I am curious why the geniuses who run these outfits keep running them into the ground just to come whining to the federal government to bail them out of the financial disasters they created. And, after which all you hear from the Republican Party is "no government interference".

I must admit, I was surprised to learn only Republican presidents gave bailouts to private enterprise. With this in mind, how is it these banks and private corporations seem to fail and need billions of taxpayer bailouts from the federal government only when there is a Republican president? Is it possible the companies deemed "too big to fail" eventually fail on purpose with cool, calculated and fine-tuned precision? For the record, *"too big to fail"* is a colloquial term describing financial institutions and private enterprises that are so large and interconnected their failure will be disastrous to the economy. And in the event they do fail, they must be rescued by the federal government. Once again, how is it these massive, mega-conglomerates only seem to fail when there is a Republican president in the oval office?

Capitalism

Growing up, I always thought "Capitalism" meant, everyone in the United States of America can make money and profit. If you got a job and got paid at the end of the week, that was capitalism at work. To a very small extent, this is true. But on a much larger scale, Capitalism is an economic system that is based on the private ownership of the means of production and the creation of goods and services for profit. Hence, the few people who own the production of goods and services capitalize and profit. Fortunately for the masses, the large corporations need to hire employees to make the process work; but as we all know, there is not enough Capitalism to go around (provide jobs for everyone in need).

During the last 30-years, give or take, a new beast has reared its ugly had under the guise of Capitalism. This beast endeavors to manipulate the U.S. economy so the nation's wealth funnels up to a very undeserving few. The new term for today is *"Vulture Capitalism"* - profit by any means necessary! When it comes to taxes, the rich does not want to pay any or as little as possible. Their main reasoning being, *"We cannot create any jobs if we're taxed to death!"* But during the 8-years of the previous George W. Bush administration, corporations got all kinds of tax breaks. And to show their appreciation, they did not hesitate to outsource U.S. jobs to overseas locations and downsize U.S. workers, accordingly.

Those tax breaks did not help create jobs; they only helped the rich keep more money/profits. Hence, they filled their bank accounts with money left over from paying fewer taxes; the savings from not doing business in the US; and, the savings from not having to pay the salaries and benefits of the American workers they downsized. The rich just got richer!

Can you now see how the corporate greedy hordes all the money to themselves? And we haven't even gotten around to those who load a company with perpetual debt and then purposely let it fail. As those in-charge load the company with debt, they line their pockets with money from loans and/or government bailouts. And the American workers are the ones who suffer the loss of jobs, salaries, benefits and pensions. But for those companies that plan to hang around, they cut/freeze salaries and pay less in salaries, benefits and taxes. If the corporations pay less in healthcare costs, more is taken out of your bi-weekly paycheck to make up the difference. Hence, more money is available in the profit margin.

In addition to outsourcing, downsizing, tax breaks and cutting salaries and benefits, the corporate greedy target the unions. What does this have to do with anything? Well, as much as unions might seem like an unnecessary pain, they have accomplished a lot over the past 100-years. And getting rid of unions means getting rid of 100-years of union achievements. Unions are responsible for just about all the things we now take for granted on our jobs:

- fair wages and relative income equality
- 8-hour work day
- Saturdays and Sundays off
- overtime pay after working 40-hours
- two 15-minute breaks every day
- one 45-minute to 1-hour lunch break every day
- worker's compensation
- employer-based healthcare coverage
- paid vacations
- paid sick days

- maternity leave
- medical leave (12-weeks unpaid)
- cost-of-living raises
- enforcing child-labor laws
- retirement plans
- safe working environments
- outlawing discrimination
- union workers make 30% more than non-union workers
- laws the protect whistle-blowers who expose corporate corruption

Even if you've never been in a union, you benefit from unions. Imagine having to go to the job you already hate without any of the benefits unions made possible over the past 100-years. On top of that, you're conditioned think union dues are for nothing. As long as these benefits exist, you have to pay a small fee for them. So, when you finally get rid of unions, you will be shocked when everything unions have achieved vanishes with them!

You think that great corporation you work for provides these things out of the kindness of their hearts? The underlying goal of the corporate greedy is to transform the work environment back to that of 100 (or more) years ago before there were unions. But the thing they're truly after is ALL THE MONEY they spend providing these benefits! If you don't like unions, you better get used to working countless mandatory hours (including Saturdays and Sundays) for less money than you currently make. And don't get sick unless you want to get fired. Oh yeah, and women, don't even think about having a baby and keeping a job.

The corporate think-tanks are light-years ahead of you on this. They spend all day every day dreaming up ways to increase their bottom-line and translate it into making YOUR life miserable. If you want to get a better idea of the environment they want to create, just start researching work environments that existed in the late 1800s and early 1900s. Prior to unions, if a worker had a complaint, it was answered later that day by a group of corporate thugs beating the complainer to near death. Can you imagine something like that happening today? The only thing stopping it is unions. But as fate would have it, we are conditioned to take things for granted and perceive unions as no longer necessary.

By now you should be able to see how hard the corporate greedy works to take more from the working class to transform into profits! Regardless to what business employers are in, the level of competition is staggering and fierce. Instead of killing themselves trying to sell more widgets, they take as much money from the expense column and transfer it to the profit margin. And guess which column contains your salary and benefits? Fewer expenses translate into bigger profits a lot easier than selling more widgets. And the groups who own the corporations love bigger profits!

In a nutshell, American capitalism is the most dynamic Pyramid scheme on the planet. In the United States, 1% of the population controls 50% of the nation's wealth while the 99% struggle over the other 50%. But schematics are being drawn up as we speak to funnel more of what the 99% fight over up to the 1%. Can you see how the 2008 collapse of the U.S. economy just might have been done on purpose? There are those who believe the Republican Party thinks collapsing the U.S. economy is good business. Is there no wonder the powers-that-be try to keep us distracted fighting over race and sexual orientation?

Capitalism is a pyramid scheme; and, like most pyramid schemes, it only benefits the ones at the top! The capitalism pyramid is maintained by thousands of smaller pyramids called, corporations; but their code for pyramid is "order-of-hierarchy". This mindset has a lot to do with why the Republican Party of Capitalism wants to keep the federal government and its rules and regulations out of private enterprise. Then, I think it's only fair that private enterprise (and presidential candidates running off experience gained in the private sector) should stay out the federal government.

Let's Talk Abortion!

For the longest I have heard Right minions screaming anti-abortion rhetoric; mostly males taking the anti-abortion stand. Why do the Rightwing minions feel so strongly about abortion? The arguments I've heard basically boil down to murdering babies! But the jury is still out on whether or not an unborn fetus constitutes a person. With this in mind, the arguments Rightwing extremists present are based on nothing more than their own personal opinions based on nothing more than their own personal opinions; no scientific evidence to back their position, at all.

The issue at hand is whether or not pregnant women have the right to choose to have an abortion or be bullied into not having an abortion by men. As matters stand at the moment, in 1976, a landmark decision was made by the Supreme Court of the United States (SCOTUS) on the issue of abortion. Roe VS Wade was decided simultaneously with a companion case, Doe VS Bolton. The Court ruled that a right to privacy under the due process clause of the 14th Amendment extended to a woman's decision to have an abortion. Howbeit, that right must be balanced against the state's two legitimate interests in regulating abortions: *protecting prenatal life and protecting women's health.* Arguing that these state interests became stronger over the course of a pregnancy, the Court ruled a woman can have an abortion up until the fetus can survive on its own outside the uterus. Whew!

There you have it! Women have the right to choose! But why do the Rightwing minions not acknowledge the Supreme Court ruling? Why do they still protest abortion and scream, holler and shout to the top of their lungs? It has been my observation, when the Rightwing minions "don't" get their way, they whine and throw hissy fits like 5-year olds. And when they do get their way, they expect everyone else to be adult about it. For example, when the SCOTUS ruled in favor of the Rightwing interpretation of the 2nd Amendment (the right to bear arms), the Rightwing minions rejoiced and everyone else just had to accept it and move on. But when the SCOTUS ruled in favor of President Obama's individual healthcare mandate, Rightwing minions whined all day, threw hissy fits and tantrums and was ready to go to war over it!

Why do Rightwing advocates feel so strong about abortions, when according to records, Republicans frequent abortion clinics to resolve their unwanted baby issues? The truth of the matter is the extreme Rightwing protest abortions until they need to have an abortion. Hence, the Rightwing minions do get abortions; they just lie about it! Then, is it possible the Rightwing powers-that-be are so anti-abortion to prevent their own minions from frequenting the abortion clinics? There might be some truth to this if the Rightwing minion army is shrinking in size. Once upon a time (over 50-years ago), Rightwing minions were plentiful enough to vote any Republican candidate into office. These days, they are considered a minority; perhaps proven by the 2012 presidential election.

Now let's see, there was Richard Nixon (1969-1974), Gerald Ford (1974-1977), Ronald Reagan (1981-1989), George H.W. Bush (1989-1993), and George W. Bush (2001-2008). Over the last 40-years, we've had five Republican presidents. There was also two Democratic presidents; Jimmy Carter (1977-1981) and Bill Clinton (1993-2001). The current President of the United States, Barack Obama (2009-Present), is a Democrat. And he has 43% of the white electorate vote to thank; many of whom were Republicans! More whites voted for Obama in 2008 than they did for John Kerry in 2004 or Al Gore in 2000. Broken down further, Barack Obama won 41% of the white female vote and 46% of white males.

Now, as Republican politicians probably already know, the white majority vote, which was once 75% of the voting pool (which includes Republican supporters), has been shrinking over the past 40-years, in direct proportion to the white majority in the general population. Since the Republican Party has depended on the white majority for so long, there's a good chance they fear their source of power if slowly but surely fading. Is this a good enough reason to be anti-abortion? Make sure those white babies-future voters get born? However, one of the main reasons pregnant women don't want to have their babies; they cannot afford to take care of them. And the Right's position against free and/or affordable healthcare does not help them get female support.

As it stands, the Right wants to force pregnant women to have babies but don't want to help take care of them, healthcare-wise. And they call President Obama a dictator? Perhaps, if the extreme Right lightened up and learned to compromise a little, abortion might not be such a controversy. If you want pregnant women to have their babies, offer them an incentive; free (or affordable) healthcare might be a good start. But the Rightwing mentality to dictate terms, take it or leave it, starts controversy and political wars. Think about it! The Right dictates no socialist (affordable or free) healthcare and they also dictate no abortions. There is one other possible reason Republicans might be so anti-abortion. The pharmaceutical industry! If the right for a woman to choose to get an abortion is completely eliminated, every single female in the country with the ability to bear children would be forced to use contraceptives. And what industry would not kill to have 50% of the country dependent on their products? These days women have a wide variety of contraceptive products to choose from:

- Birth Control Pills
- Birth Control Implants
- Birth Control Patches
- Birth Control Shots
- Birth Control Injections
- Morning After Pill
- Hormone Pills
- The IUD (Intrauterine Device)
- Essure (non-surgical, hormone-free, permanent birth control procedure)
- Cervical Cap (with Spermicide)
- Diaphragm (with Spermicide)
- NuvaRing
- Hysterectomy
- Female Condoms
- Vibrators (?)

Is it possible the Pharmaceutical Industry is the driving force behind Rightwing hostility towards abortion? In a nutshell, they send lobbyists to Congress; who then courts Rightwing politicians; who start their anti-abortion campaigns; and Fox News spreads the message to its viewers. Howbeit, they deliver the message under the guise of "Christianity". The Rightwing minions proceed to perceive religion as nothing more than a license to be evil.

Gay Marriage (The Religious View)

Gay marriage is one of the hottest topics of debate. How hot is it? It is so hot, the Rightwing minions pretend they are Christians! Some of them even start quoting Bible verses. Or should I say, misquoting Bible verses out-of-context. You know if they involve God, or their version of God who is a bigot just like they are, they don't really have an argument. Bible verses the Rightwing minions purport condemns homosexuality appear to be the only biblical texts they are familiar with. With this in mind, to them the Bible is nothing more than a tool they use to try to bully and intimidate other (Gay) people out of their civil rights. Hence, Rightwing advocates assume everyone believes-in the Bible.

The harsh reality is that "nobody" really obeys the Bible, so why keep bringing it up? For instance, the Bible says, "Thou shalt not kill". But the reason none of us have killed anyone is not because the Bible tells us not to, as much as, we have no reason to. And even if we did have a reason, we don't do it because we might either get the death penalty or life in prison. But in their defense, the Rightwing minions never profess to be Christians; they profess to have "religious beliefs". Having religious beliefs is the practice of making everyone else "assume" you are a Christian. But (some) laws are based on "religious beliefs", not the fact you actually practice a religion. Hence, the Rightwing minions who profess to have religious beliefs can do so without having to change a thing about themselves, as Christianity requires.

Leviticus 18:22
The Rightwing minions have convenient religious beliefs when the topic is gay marriage. Time after time, they repeat the same old Bible verses, howbeit out-of-context, taken from the Book of Leviticus in the Old Testament. On that note, the Book of Leviticus was addressed to the ancient Hebrew tribe of Levi. Get it? LEVI-ticus. In Greek, the suffix "ticus" is the same as the English "tical". In essence, the book is Levi-tical; pertaining to the Levites/Tribe of Levi. FYI: Levi was one out of twelve Hebrew tribes; they were considered the priest tribe of the Hebrew race. Hence, the priestly tribe of Levi was held at a much higher standard than the other eleven tribes; spelled out in the Book of Leviticus.

The Rightwing minions learn to surgically extract a specific Bible verse, then quote it out-of-context, forcing their own meaning and interpretation onto the text. And when they repeat this process enough times, they begin to actually believe they're quoting what God wrote. For instance, Leviticus 18:22 reads:

> **Thou shalt not lie with <u>mankind</u>, as with womankind: it [is] abomination.**

They then claim "God" calls homosexuality an abomination, not us! But does the text even mention homosexuality? Is it at all talking about homosexuality? Are homosexuals the only men who lie with other men as with a woman? Of course not! One has to put the text back in its proper context to fully understand it. The previous verse, Leviticus 18:21, says:

> **And thou shalt not let any of thy seed pass through *the fire* to Molech, neither shalt thou profane the name of thy God: I *am* the LORD.**

In its proper context, the Levitical priests (Levites) were told not to act like those who worshipped, Molech. The Molechian priests sacrificed children in fire and had sexual intercourse with male humans and beasts in the temple. Take note that the English word *"mankind"* of verse-22, taken from the Hebrew *"zakar (zah-KHAR)"*, more accurately means *"male-kind"*. It is not exclusive to humans! However, the English word *"womankind"* taken from the Hebrew *"ishshah (eesh-SHAH)"* is exclusive to female humans. Its opposite is *"iysh (EESH)"*, exclusively pertaining to male humans. So, if the text of Leviticus 18:22 exclusively referred to men having sex with other men, it would have used the word *"iysh* (male humans).

Another Rightwing minion asked, *"What about the Old Testament story of Sodom and Gomorrah?"* Well, we don't know much about Gomorrah other than it was destroyed. But the Rightwing minions assume both cities were destroyed because they were filled with homosexuals. Hence, God destroyed these cities because he hates homosexuals! OK. If this were true, why was the righteous Lot and his family living in Sodom if the place was one enormous Gay parade? Rightwing minions claim it is God who hates homosexuals, not them! But do the Rightwing minions give the impression "they" are God's representatives on earth?

Genesis 19

Now let me get this straight (no pun intended), the Rightwing minions think God hates homosexuals because of a 5000-year old story they interpret to mean: *God destroyed the small town of Sodom with fire and brimstone because it was full of homosexuals?*

Then how do they interpret the story where God destroyed an entire planet full of heterosexuals with a flood? A whole family of heterosexuals survived aboard an ark? What makes you so sure no one in that family was gay? After all, homosexuals are still here!

The Rightwing minions conclude, the mob outside of Lot's front door did not accept the women he offered them in the place of males they targeted. Hence, the mob must have been gay! Is this the only reason a mob full of men would reject a female offering to do with sexually as they pleased? No! Consider the attitude that men in prisons an penitentiaries have when new inmates arrive. Most of them salivate over the possibility of sexually assaulting the new arrivals in a blind rage! This is the same mentality the men outside Lot's front door had. It had nothing at all to do with homosexuality as much as it did, wickedness!

As a matter of fact, a similar story is found in Judges 19. The same type of mob demanded the male behind the locked door. And as this story turned out, in this case, the mod accepted the female instead of their would-be male victim. In the Genesis 19 story, Lot offered the mob his daughters because he knew there was a chance the mob would accept his daughters and leave his male guests in peace. This makes no sense if the mob consisted of homosexuals. And once again, why was Lot living among Gay people unless he, himself, enjoyed their company?

Romans 1:26-27

Homosexuality is unnatural? If I had a dollar for every time I heard this one... Homosexuals have existed since the beginning of the human race. At what point are they not "natural" by now? Homosexuality might not be the "natural sexual behavior" for heterosexuals but neither is heterosexuality the "natural sexual behavior" for homosexuals. Now, can we call it even? Another Rightwing advocate hit me with Romans 1:26-27:

> For this cause God gave them up unto vile affections: for even their women did change the natural use into that which is against nature:

> And likewise also the men, leaving the natural use of the woman, burned in their lust one toward another; men with

**men working that which is unseemly, and receiving in
themselves that recompense of their error which was meet.**

Once again, the text is surgically extracted and quoted out-of-context. The subject matter actually begins at verse 18:

**For the wrath of God is revealed from heaven against all
ungodliness and unrighteousness of men, who hold the truth
in unrighteousness;**

Yes, this text is referring to everybody! ALL ungodliness and ALL unrighteousness! This even includes the actions and deeds of the Rightwing minions who never consider what God thinks of their behavior. But they think homosexuals should consider what they (Rightwing advocates) purport God thinks of them (homosexuals).

Romans 1:26 talks about women who changed the "natural use" into that which is against nature. Does this refer to Lesbianism? On the contrary, Lesbians existed in every culture and society thousands of years before this text was written! How were they not considered a natural part of the human race by the time this text was written? The crux of the text is the "*natural use of a woman.*" What exactly is that? *Child bearing!* How do women go against their own nature of getting pregnant after having sex? I'm sure at the time they had methods but in modern times we have:

- Birth Control Pills
- Birth Control Implants
- Birth Control Patches
- Birth Control Shots
- Morning After Pill
- The IUD (Intrauterine Device)
- Essure (non-surgical, hormone-free, permanent birth control procedure)
- Cervical Cap
- Diaphragm
- Hysterectomy
- Female Condoms
- Masturbation
- Oral Sex
- Anal Sex
- Vibrators
- Sex Dolls

- Abortions

Now, should we all freak out and start protesting pharmaceutical companies that provide contraceptives or should we make a conscious decision to either agree or disagree with the opinion of the guy who wrote the text in Romans?

Verse 27 is also taken completely out-of-context to make it appear the topic is gay men. When men leave the natural use of a woman, which is to have sex and bear children, they use birth control methods to prevent the woman from doing what she would naturally do after having sex; get pregnant. Men burned in their lust to have sex with women without suffering the consequences, just like they do today. Men with men working that which is unseemly is not referring to homosexuality! It is referring to men with men (collaborating) on ways to prevent women from getting pregnant. THIS is what the New Testament deems unnatural!

Gay Marriage (The Political View)

Homosexuals are 3% of the population?
If this were true, gay people would still be in the closet! In addition to that, they probably would not be winning so many political victories on the gay marriage front! Eight years ago, there was no such thing as gay marriage in the United States. Today, gay marriage is legal in nearly half the country! The Rightwing minions claim gay people are 3% of the U.S. population. That's is about 9.5-million out of about 315-million people! Spread across 50 states that's about 189,000 homosexuals per state or 1% of each state's population. Do you honestly think these trivial numbers would be winning so big, politically across the country?

Surveys taken over 50-years ago when homosexuals were still in the closet concluded homosexuals comprised as much as 20% of the U.S. population. That was over 35-million people in the 1960s! In 1948, author Alfred Kinsey shocked the world when he stated in his book, *Sexual Behavior in the Human Male,* that 10% of the male population was gay. Now, with all things being equal, if 10% of women were also gay at the time would that add up to 20% of the population as far back as 1948? During that time, the U.S.

population was around 146.6-million. This equates to around 29.3-million homosexuals in American society in 1948. But the truth of the matter is that no one will ever know for sure how much of the population is gay. But rest assured, if any survey claims an extremely low number (i.e. 1% to 4%), it is completely biased against homosexuals.

With this in mind, Gary Gates of the Williams Institute conducted a review in April 2011 that concluded approximately 3.8% of American adults identify themselves either as lesbian or gay. Was he being generous? Now, Gary Gates holds a lot of credentials:
- a PhD in Public Policy; Heinz School of Public Policy & Mngmt, Carnegie Mellon University
- a Master of Divinity degree; St. Vincent College
- a BS in Computer Science; University of Pittsburgh at Johnstown

So, why would his conclusions be so different than other surveys that say the complete opposite? For instance, an August 2002 Gallup survey concluded 21% of males are gay and 22% of females are lesbians. Is this the same as saying over 40% of the U.S. population is gay? In 2011, the U.S. population was about 311.8-million. Gates' conclusions suggested only 11.8-million were gay. In 2002, the U.S. population was about 287.4-million. If half were male, 143.7-million @ 21% would equal 30.2-million. And if half were female, 143.7-million @ 22% would equal 31.6-million. Now, when we add these two figures together we get 61.8-million gay people in the United States.

Other more recent surveys conclude 1 in every 5 people in the United States is gay. This would amount to about 63-million people (20% of the current population). Similar surveys conclude 1 in every 4 people in the United States is gay. This would amount to 78.8-million people (25% of the current population). Be that as it may, President Obama acknowledged six months before the 2012 presidential election (when he endorsed gay marriage), gay people are a very large and powerful voting bloc! It's too bad the other guy was too wrapped up in his own party's rhetoric to even remotely consider gaining this edge among registered voters. As fate would have it, the more open-minded guy won the election and the close-minded guy never knew what hit him. The anti-gay advocates lean towards Gary Gate's claim that gay people are a very small minority (3.8%) but the more open-minded and rational people can look around and realize there are a lot more gay people than Gary Gates claims!

Homosexuals Are The Moral Decay Of Society?
According to common sense, heterosexuals commit murder, rape, incest, lie, cheat, steal, con, deceive, misled, distort, manipulate, bully, intimidate, serial kill, serial rape, wife beat, child beat, child molest, kidnap, verbally abuse, rob banks, embezzle, identity theft, stalk, cyber bully, betray, divorce and outright terrorize other people but homosexuals are the moral decay of society?

Homosexuals Are Mentally Ill?
This argument comes from people who are bigots, but were not born bigots; instead were conditioned, groomed and programmed to be bigots, and having the audacity to question someone else's mental health. When talking about mental health, let's what the professionals have to say on the subject:

- The American Medical Association
- The American Psychiatric Association
- The American Psychological Association
- The American Psychoanalytic Association
- The American Academy of Pediatrics
- The National Association of Social Workers

All of these professional organizations who deal with mental health issues on a daily basis say, *"Homosexuality is NOT a mental disorder and oppose attempts at reparative or conversion therapy. Sexual orientation is NOT a choice and cannot be changed."*

Jesus Never Mentioned Homosexuality?
Most would-be Bible scholars share this conclusion. But what they all have in common is not knowing the biblical language the New Testament uses when referring to homosexuals or homosexuality. To moment you learn to speak biblical language, the sooner you will comprehend when the Bible is referring to homosexuals. For instance, recorded in Matthew 19:12:

> **For there are some eunuchs, which were so born from [their] mother's womb: and there are some eunuchs, which**

were made eunuchs of men: and there be eunuchs, which have made themselves eunuchs for the kingdom of heaven's sake. He that is able to receive [it], let him receive [it].

Let's begin with that last statement, "He that is able to receive this, let him receive it!" Obviously, close-minded people existed even back then and were anticipated. Now, the key word is *"eunuchs"*. The common assumption in the western world is that eunuchs were heterosexual men who had their genitals or testicles removed via a medical procedure. Why would such a feat be necessary? To perform a certain functions; typically, to oversee harems (the multiple wives of a very wealthy man). A strong man (slave) was castrated so he could oversee the harem without getting physically involved with the harem. Hence, this manmade version of a eunuch produced a man who was not sexually attracted to women. Typically, this was the whole point of being a eunuch.

The text lists three different types of eunuchs in order of the most to the least common. The text reveals, the most common type of eunuch was born a eunuch. Does this suggest there was a segment of the male population born castrated? If so, how would you tell a male child born castrated from a female child? Yes! This idea is preposterous! One the contrary, some eunuchs were born males who were naturally not sexually attracted to females. Can we identify any group of people who fit this description? Yes! We call them "homosexuals" but the New Testament calls them "eunuchs". Now, whenever you see this word (eunuch) in the Bible, you know the type of person it's referring to; men born from their mother's womb with no sexual desire to be with a woman.

Natural eunuchs were often considered spiritually gifted people. There are many examples covered-up in the Bible. Joseph and his Technicolor Dream Coat would today be considered a Drag Queen. Regardless of his sexual nature, he was considered the most gifted interpreter of dreams in Egypt! Before you traditionalist get all bent out of shape, the coat given to Joseph by his father, who knew him very well, was a garment only worn by female royalty. Even then this type of individual was considered a "Queen". Joseph's brothers hated him because he was among the youngest of twelve brothers but their father treated him like the eldest. A special gift, such as a Technicolor Dream Coat, would be from the father to his eldest son who was first in the line of inheritance.

The second most common type of eunuch were those made so by men. As previously mentioned, this was done by various forms of castration. Often after one empire conquered another empire, many of the young men of royalty were taken captive and made into eunuchs to serve in their new king's court. Now, depending on the service they would provide, different types of castration was performed. In addition to duties during the day, the various types of castration dictated their activity at night:

- a masculine guard to oversee the harem (and not be tempted)
- a masculine sex toy for the harem (and not procreate)
- an effeminate sex toy specifically for the king
- an effeminate sex toy who served palace officials

Finally, the text in Matthew mentions the third, least common, type of eunuch. Men who devoted their lives to God, who made a conscious decision to be castrated so they would not be distracted by worldly lust for (and attraction to) the opposite sex.

God made Adam & Eve; Not Adam & Steve?
Actually, God made Adam, without Eve! The creature called Adam was isolated in the garden of Eden for an unspecified amount of time before Eve was created. This detail suggests Adam "was not" initially intended to be a heterosexual. Otherwise, he would have instantly been created male and female like every other mammal.

Genesis 2:18-20:

> **And the LORD God said, [It is] not good that the man should be alone; I will make for him an help meet. Then out of the ground the LORD God formed every beast of the field ... to see what the man would call them ... And Adam gave names to all cattle, fowl and beast of the field; but for Adam there was not found an help meet among them.**

This version of the story is watered down but it is not that difficult to see what was really going on if you don't stray from the crux. After the man was created, it took a while for the LORD to realize he should not be alone and isolated. But what did he do to remedy the situation? Make a bunch of animals and keep the man so busy he would forget all about being alone? On the contrary, the "giving of names" in this situation was more like "pet names" after mating. He didn't call the cow a Cow; he named the cow he got intimate with, "Chelsea". He didn't call the sheep a Sheep; he named the sheep he got intimate with, "Lucy". The text ends on the same note it began, none of the new animals were sexually compatible. At this point, you might want to consider the possibility those:

- **Centaur** (half-man/half-horse)
- **Malion** (half-man/half-lion)
- **Satyr** (half-man/half-goat)
- **Minotaur** (half-man/half-bull)
- **Griffin** (half-man/half-eagle)

were the result of the man in the garden mating with the animals in the garden. And once upon a time the creatures now considered mythical, did actually once upon a time roam the earth.

Redefining Marriage, Seriously?

Murderers and Serial Killers serving a life sentence in prison and/or are on Death Row are free to get married if they so choose but law-abiding homosexuals cannot? This is the epitome of a double-standard! Gay people work jobs, start businesses, vote in public elections, entertain, invent, create, fight in our armed services, police our streets, teach our children, and excel in sporting events, but they are not free to legally wed (each other) if they so choose? This, to me sounds a lot like "exploitation". To counter-argue, the Rightwing minions claim gay people want to redefine marriage! But the way I see it, heterosexuals have redefined marriage dozens of times. So, why tighten your panties over one more definition?

- **Monogamy** : a person is allowed only one spouse
- **Bigamy** : a person has more than one spouse (non-consensual)
- **Polygamy** : a person has more than one spouse (consensual)
- **Polygyny** : a man has more than one wife
- **Polyandry** : a woman has more than one husband
- **Polyamory** : members of a group are married to each other
- **Open** : the partners agree that each may engage in extramarital sexual relationships

- **Henogamy** : exactly one of the children (or male children) in a family can marry
- **Arranged** : parents of bride agree with parents of groom, their children will marry each other
- **Bilateral Cross Cousin** : two men marry each other's sisters
- **Matrilateral Cross Cousin** : a man is expected to marry his mother's brother's daughter
- **Patrilateral Cross Cousin** : a man is expected to marry his father's sister's daughter
- **Levirate** : a man marries the widow of his deceased brother
- **Sororate** : a widowed man marries one of his deceased wife's sisters; most likely the next eldest
- **Hypergyny** : a woman marries up (socially speaking)
- **Hypogyny** : a woman marries down (socially speaking)
- **Common Law** : the oldest form of marriage - predates religion: two people lived together for so long, they consider themselves married
- **Endogamy** : limiting marriages within certain social groups, ethnicities, or classes
- **Exogamy** : marriage outside a social group, clan, class
- **Mixed** : marriage between people of two different religions/races
- **Egalitarian** : husband and wife are considered equal partners

Homosexuals Can't Reproduce?

I, for one, have never heard homosexuals claim they want the right to reproduce. This argument stems from the only commandment during the creation period that God gave to mankind:

> **And God blessed them, and God said unto them, Be fruitful, and multiply, and replenish the earth.** [Genesis 1:28]

Some of the Rightwing minions claim this was God's commandment for heterosexuals to get married! But I see God telling a bunch of naked people to have sex and make babies with no stipulations. Unfortunately, the people who dictate all the rules can't have it that simple! Be that as it may, when millions of heterosexual couples cannot reproduce; they adopt! Marriage is not a commandment sent down from the throne of heaven. As a matter of fact, the Bible only "talks about" marriage and people who were married; it never actually tells people to get married.

Early societies were male oriented. Hence, homosexual men had the same rights and privileges as heterosexual men. And wealthy homosexual men had wives, children and harems (a display of status) no different than their heterosexual counterparts. The only real difference was the fact that homosexual men had male lovers in the same capacity that heterosexual men had mistresses. As long as men in general had all the rights and privileges, there was nothing in these societies to encourage homosexuals to want to marry each other. Finally, in the text of Genesis 1:28, sexual orientation is not specified. All humans were commanded to be fruitful and multiply. To suggest "all humans" at the time were heterosexuals (especially with no proof) is just plain dumb.

Rightwing Christianity

An extremely mean-spirited, nasty, and hostile threw the following biblical text in my face claiming God hates gay people. But as I actually read the text (something they obviously did not do), I realized it did Identify a specific group of people; but it was not gay people. 1Timothy 3:1-5 reads:

> This know also, that in the <u>last days</u> perilous times shall come. For <u>men shall be lovers of their own selves</u>, covetous, boasters, proud, blasphemers, disobedient to parents, unthankful, unholy, <u>Without natural affection</u>, trucebreakers, false accusers, incontinent, fierce, despisers of those that are good, Traitors, heady, high-minded, lovers of pleasures more than lovers of God; Having a <u>form of godliness</u>, <u>but denying the power thereof</u>: from such turn away.

I can see how surgically extracting bits and pieces of this text can give a false impression it is talking about homosexuality, but the Rightwing minions are programmed "not" to read the whole thing. First, the underlined *"last days"* does not refer to the "end of the world" as much as it refers to the "*end of an age (a period in time)".* The next underlined text, *"men shall be lovers of their own selves"* does not refer to "men having sex with men" as much as it does *"driven by self-interests at the expense of others", "money loving", "empty pretenders", "braggarts", "slanderous", "non-compliant to rules, regulations and laws for no apparent reason".*

The next underlined text *"Without natural affection"* does not refer to "homosexuality" as much as it refers to *"lacking brotherly love"*. And this unnatural state exhibits *trucebreakers* (hostile protesters), *false accusers* (lying, deceiving, distorting, misrepresenting), *incontinent* (letting hostile emotions dictate their actions), *fierce* (hostile), and *despisers of those that are good* (based on race, religion, politics), *treacherous, heady* (reckless behavior), *high-minded* (blinded by own views), *loving how this behavior makes them feel more than how obeying God makes them feel,* and *having a form of godliness* (calling themselves "Christians") but *denying the power thereof* (but not practicing Christianity). The Rightwing minions are quick to claim this text refers to gay people because it actually describes the Rightwing minions to the tee!

No Compromise?

The Rightwing minions don't want any other group to get anything they want when it falls outside Rightwing social views. Hence, society should conform only to the likes and dislikes of the Rightwing minions. But my suspicions is they are told what to like and dislike by the powers-that-be (Heritage Foundation, Fox News, Freedomworks). There is always a method behind the madness! When one group wants something that will interfere with their agenda, the Rightwing minions don't hesitate to form hostile would-be lynch mobs under the guise of protesting.

The basic Rightwing attitude is "no compromise". In other words, they refuse to compromise on any issue that contradicts their own views. What they don't seem to realize is the fact one has to be in a position of absolute power and hold all the cards in order to not compromise. Hence, the Rightwing minions claim they won't compromise on issues where they have no power or influence. For example, President Obama's healthcare law; the Rightwing minions never held anything of value that would put them in a position to compromise or not. As a result, they created chaos and wreaked havoc on all of society, like going on strike! Well, they, themselves, didn't go on strike; they forced 800,000 federal employees to go on strike (for 16-days) by filibustering the Republican controlled House of Representatives, forcing them to miss the October 1st FY2014 Spending Bill deadline.

What the Tea Party calls *"not compromising"* is what rational people call *"throwing a hissy fit and tantrum"*. In September 2013, the Tea Party demanded President Obama negotiate the 3-year old healthcare law (Affordable Care Act/Obamacare). This bill had already been negotiated and signed into law in March 2010. The Tea Party was making a demand about an issue they had no control or influence over. In addition, President Obama was not obligated to RE-negotiate the 3-year old healthcare law while the Tea Party and the rest of Congress was suppose to be negotiating the FY2014 Spending Bill. Hence, the Tea Party's idea of not compromising boiled down to them refusing to do the jobs they were sent to Congress to do; and making sure every other civilian federal employee refused to their jobs! In other words, the Tea Party forced all civilian federal employees to go on strike.

Now, this was an interesting course of action since the Tea Party and every other Republican is always trying to annihilate Labor Unions and eliminate Bargaining Rights to prevent employees in the private sector from ever going on strike! The Rightwing minion's concept of "no compromise" was actually an ultimatum! If the president did not give-in to the Tea Party's ridiculous demand to include the 3-year old Affordable Care Act law in the FY2014 Spending Bill negotiations, they would cause a work stoppage in the federal government. President Obama, being the rational and level-headed person he is, stepped back and let the Tea Party run its course. Hence, 800,000 federal employees were forced to stay home for 16-days while the Tea Party slowly realized their stunt was not accomplishing anything they wanted it to accomplish.

Insanity
The definition of *"insanity"* is *"doing the same thing over again and expecting different results"*.

In 1996, Republicans shut down the federal government in an attempt "to force" President Clinton to sign their spending bill (that only benefited rich people). After the 21-day shutdown concluded:

- Republicans found most of the country against them;
- the Republican Party was a complete laughing stock;
- House Speaker Newt Gingrich was portrayed as a whining baby by the media; and

- Republicans wound up signing Bill Clinton's spending bill

In 2013, Congressional Republicans (mainly the Tea Party element) shut down the federal government in an attempt "to force" President Obama to RE-negotiate the Affordable Care Act (aka Obamacare) that was already negotiated and signed into law 3-years prior. After a 16-day shutdown concluded:

- Republicans found most of the country against them;
- The Republican Party was a complete laughing stock, again;
- House Speaker John Boehner was portrayed as a whining baby by the media;
- Republicans wound up signing the Democratic Senate's (aka President Obama's) spending bill; and
- Obamacare emerged unscathed

That 2nd Amendment Thing

Rightwing advocates are so passionate about gun control, they are willing to change the meaning of the U.S. Constitution. But as I said before, there is always a method behind the madness! In April 2013, the U.S. Senate voted 54-46 to expand background checks for gun buyers after the Newtown school massacre of December 2012. But unfortunately, the bill required 60-votes to pass the Senate. The Rightwing minions danced the jig for the next 5-months when they ran smack into the FY2014 Spending Bill negotiations where they expected President Obama to forget all about what happened with gun control and how they responded, and allow them to dismantle his healthcare plan.

Why are the Rightwing minions so adamant about gun control laws, or the lack thereof when most of them don't even own a gun? Once again, they are only doing what they are told to do! By who? The National Rifle Association (NRA), a lobbyist group for the gun industry and gun manufacturers. The people who run the gun industry are typical Rightwing-minded individuals who want what all Republicans want; no federal regulations interfering with their ability to generate as many profits as they possibly can! Yes, gun control laws are "federal regulations" within the gun industry. And the few the federal regulations, the freer the gun industry will be to sell guns to whoever they want, including your children.

In 2004, President Bush and the Republican Congress allowed the "1994 Federal Ban on Assault Weapons" expire. For the record, they later had to deal with the Obama administration when the Bush tax breaks were scheduled to expire at the end of 2010. But the midterms favored Republicans granting them control of the House of Representatives and six seats in the Senate. The 42 Republicans in the Senate pledged to block all legislation until the Bush tax cuts were extended. Another sign, Republicans only want what Republicans only want. But in an effort to avoid letting American families become collateral damage from congressional bickering, President Obama appointed two bi-partisan officers to oversee a deal to extend the Bush tax cuts.

Once again, gun control laws regulate the manufacture, sale, transfer, possession, modification, and use of firearms. The gun powers-that-be go to great lengths to limit laws that will limit gun sales. One method to gain support is to convince the Rightwing minions that owning a gun is their constitutional right supported by the 2nd Amendment. Even though most minions don't own a gun, they take pride in quoting the five words of the 2nd Amendment they purport grants them the right to own a gun. This pleasure stems from their desire to challenge President Obama any chance they get and prevent him from achieving his goals.

The actual 2nd Amendment consists of 27 words:

A well regulated Militia, being necessary to the security of a free State, the right of the people to keep and bear arms, shall not be infringed.

But the Rightwing version only consists of FIVE words:

The right to bear arms!

And when challenged, they recite the extended version:

The right of the people to keep and bear arms, shall not be infringed.

In essence, they will manipulate the text in any way possible to force it to agree with their belief, they have a constitutional right to own firearms! But why does owning firearms have to be a constitutional right? To give the impression gun control is illegal! But if owning guns were a constitutional right:

- State Gun Laws would be unconstitutional and illegal
- There would be federal programs giving away free guns to poor people
- None of the states could require you to have a "Gun Permit"
- There would be a Public Option for less expensive guns
- The Rightwing minions would be whining, "President Obama is forcing us to buy our own guns!"
- "Gun Free Zones" would be unconstitutional and illegal
- None of the states could force you to take a 14-hour course, pass a written test, pass a shooting test, then submit a Firearm Permit application (or any variation thereof). Instead, you could just waltz on down to the nearest gun shop and buy a gun over the counter with no questions asked.
- Every business would be selling guns; like slot machines in Las Vegas
- A license would not be required to sell guns
- States could require a Background Check, Criminal Investigation or any other kind of check as long as you're a US citizen
- States could require you to have a "concealed weapons" permit
- There would never have been a Federal Ban on Assault Weapons (1994-2004) or a Gun Control Act passed in 1968
- Guns would never have had to be "invented"; we'd all be born with a gun in our hands
- Gun Control would never be a debate (or vote) in Congress
- there would be "government guns" like there's "government cheese"
- Every Republican in the country would've been screaming about their 2nd Amendment Rights violation when Bill Clinton enacted a Federal Ban on Assault Weapons in 1994

When the NRA wants to generate gun sales, they get Republican politicians to go on FOX NEWS and announce, *"President Obama is attacking your 2nd Amendment right to bear arms!"* The next day, the minions rush out to the gun stores and empty the shelves! At the end of the day, the NRA, gun manufacturers, gun store owners, and Republican politicians laugh all the way to the bank!

The Militia, The Right Of The People!

The 2nd Amendment begins by telling us what it's talking about, "A well regulated militia". The Oxford English dictionary (the authority on definitions) defines the term, *"to bear arms"*, to mean: *To serve as a soldier, do military service, and fight.* This 1330 definition is what the 2nd Amendment written in 1791 was based on. It was not based on 2009 Rightwing propaganda; private gun ownership.

Now, the text must be read in the way it was written in the 16th century, in order to fully understand it. For instance, the Preamble begins, *"WE THE PEOPLE, in order to form a more perfect union, establish justice ..."* It is typically assumed *"We the people"* refers to every U.S. citizen. But was every U.S. citizen present in the room when the document was being written? Hence, can *"We the people"* exclusively refer to the group of people who were present while the document was being written and signed? In like manner, the 2nd Amendment uses the phrase, "the people" to exclusively refer to "the people in the militia" it identifies at the beginning. In other words, the militia is the people who have the right to keep and bear arms; and that is the exact description of a militia!

The people in general have the right to have a militia serve as the first line of defense when a foreign military decides to invade. This was enacted on the midnight-morn of April 19, 1775, when Paul Revere rode through town alerting the Colonial militia, *"The Regulars (British) are coming! The Regulars (British) are coming!"* After the American Revolutionary War was over, the debate of whether to have a standing army or militias emerged. The one main advantage of a militia was it could quickly muster to fight off an invasion. But a standing trained military had the advantage on the battlefield where militias were known to not stand their ground. As a matter of fact, records of the constitutional debate over the early drafts of the language of the 2nd Amendment included significant discussion of whether service in the militia should be compulsory (mandatory) for all able bodied men or an exemption for the religiously scrupulous conscientious objector.

Regardless to how the Rightwing minions are programmed to dissect the text of the 2nd Amendment to force their own meaning regarding private gun ownership, the historical records support the fact it was written specifically about militias. Be that as it may, some Rightwing minions claim every U.S. citizen is the militia who is to be armed to protect themselves from a tyrannical government. In other words, the Rightwing minions think when the government was being formed, it was so concerned about becoming tyrannical (something that had never happened, hence why the concern?) that they left instructions for all the citizens to arm themselves and overthrow the government. This had to be the only government in the history of governments to leave itself wide-open and openly invite a coup. Then why have public elections if people can just arm themselves and overthrow the government?

In conclusion, the 2nd Amendment was written by *James Madison*, one of the 55 delegates to attend the *Philadelphia Constitutional Convention* of 1787. The document was presented to the House of Representatives on June 8, 1789, and ratified on December 15, 1791. And not once did James Madison claim he wrote the 2nd Amendment so the people can arm themselves and overthrow a tyrannical government. On that note, if we truly had a *"tyrannical government"* the people would not bother trying to interpret the 2nd Amendment before they rebelled! Case and point, the 2nd Amendment did not exist in 1776 when the militias armed themselves to fight the British. They just did it!

In Conclusion
We have traced the Rightwing movement through the following political trek:

- Democratic-Republican Party (1791-1825)
- National Republican Party, southern-based (1825-1833)
- Whig Party (1833-1860)
- (National) Democratic Party, northern-based (1855-1860)
- Southern Democratic Party (1860)
- Southern Confederate Democrats (1861-1865)
- Democratic Party [the southern element] (1866-1947)
- State's Rights Democratic Party (1948-1948)
- The Democratic Party [politicians only] (1949-Present)
- The Republican Party [all the minions] (1949-Present)

Good Hunting!

Wikipedia Searches

- First Party System
- Democratic-Republican Party
- Republicanism in the United States
- Jeffersonian Democracy
- Federalist Party
- Alexander Hamilton
- James Monroe
- John Quincy Adams
- William H. Crawford
- Henry Clay
- National Democratic Party (United States)
- Democratic Party (United States)
- Republican Party (United States)
- Radical Republicans
- Whig Party (United States)
- Stephen A. Douglas
- Abraham Lincoln
- Constitutional Union Party (United States)
- Confederate States of America
- American Civil War
- Ulysses S. Grant
- Robert E. Lee
- John Wilkes Booth
- One-drop rule
- Ku Klux Klan
- Carpetbagger
- Scalawag
- Rutherford B. Hayes
- Samuel J. Tilden
- Compromise of 1877
- States' Rights Democratic Party
- Harry S. Truman
- Storm Thurmond
- Dixiecrat
- President's Committee on Civil Rights
- Civil Rights Movement
- Brown v. Board of Education
- Plessy v. Ferguson
- Separate But Equal
- Emmett Till
- Rosa Parks
- Montgomery Improvement Association
- Martin Luther King, Jr.
- Fred Shuttlesworth
- Southern Christian Leadership Conference
- Orval Faubus

- Little Rock Nine
- Congress of Racial Equality
- Student Nonviolent Coordinating Committee
- James Meredith
- Eugene "Bull" Connor
- Medger Evers
- NAACP
- I Have A Dream
- 16th Street Baptist Church bombing
- Lyndon B. Johnson
- Civil Rights Act of 1964
- Fox News Channel
- Keith Rupert Murdoch
- News of the World
- The Sun (United Kingdom)
- Media Matters for America
- Anita Dunn
- Nielsen ratings
- National Debt
- Medicare (United States)
- Gross Domestic Product
- Debt-to-GDP ratio
- Bureau of Labor Statistics
- Troubled Asset Relief Program
- Barack Obama
- George W. Bush
- Bill Clinton
- George H. W. Bush
- Ronald Reagan
- Jimmy Carter
- Gerald Ford
- Richard Nixon
- Diane Sawyer
- Mitch McConnell
- ATF gunwalking scandal
- Eric Holder
- House Oversight Committee
- 2012 Benghazi attack
- Barbara Boxer
- Mitt Romney
- Great Depression
- Roaring Twenties
- Warren G. Harding
- Calvin Coolidge
- Herbert Hoover
- Franklin D. Roosevelt
- New Deal

- Glass–Steagall Act of 1932
- Carter Glass
- Henry B. Steagall
- United States Debt-Ceiling Crisis Of 2011
- United States Debt-Ceiling Crisis Of 2013
- United States Federal Budget
- Budget Sequestration In 2013
- Community Reinvestment Act
- Savings And Loan Crisis
- NAFTA
- Trade and Tariff Act of 1984
- Brian Mulroney
- Carlos Salinas de Gortari
- Gramm–Leach–Bliley Act
- Phil Gramm
- Jim Leach
- Thomas J. Bliley, Jr.
- Presidency of Bill Clinton
- Newt Gingrich
- United States Federal Government Shutdowns of 1995 and 1995–96
- Congressional Research Service
- Obamacare
- Patient Protection and Affordable Care Act
- Consolidated Omnibus Budget Reconciliation Act of 1985
- National Socialist German Workers' Party
- Socialized Medicine
- American Medical Association
- Operation Coffee Cup
- Community organizing
- Sarah Palin
- Developing Communities Project
- Food Stamp Act of 1964
- Laissez-Faire
- Capitalism
- Vulture Capitalism
- Welfare
- Aid to Families with Dependent Children
- Supplemental Nutrition Assistance Program
- Reconstruction Finance Corporation
- National Welfare Rights Organization
- Abortion in the United States
- Abortion debate
- Roe v. Wade
- Same-sex marriage
- Second Amendment to the United States Constitution
- Militia (United States)

www.ingramcontent.com/pod-product-compliance
Lightning Source LLC
Chambersburg PA
CBHW020442290526
45785CB00002B/982